THE JOHNSON

COUNTY MURDERS

THE TRUE STORY OF AN INDIANA TRIAL FOR TRIPLE MURDER

John R Berger

1

THE AUTHOR: The author is a graduate of Hillsdale College and Harvard Law School. He is a retired judge of the Steuben Circuit Court and Professor Emeritus of Law at Tri-State University. He is the author of two additional books, his autobiography, *The Bubbles Rise*, a sentimental journey told with humor and poignancy, and *Change of Venue,* a survey of law textbook which incorporates the triple murder trial featured in *The Johnson County Murders.*

Copyright 2016 by John R. Berger   Comments welcomed at jrb11129@yahoo.com

Published 2016 by Lake James Press
20 Lane 200H Lake James
Angola, Indiana 46703

STATE OF INDIANA

SUPREME COURT

RANDALL T. SHEPARD, CHIEF JUSTICE

304 STATE HOUSE

INDIANAPOLIS 46204-2798

March 9, 2010

Hon. John R. Berger
20 LN 200H LK James
Angola, Indiana 46703

Dear Judge Berger:

Thanks so much for sending along a copy of your book "The Johnson County Murders", which I have enjoyed. It is a gripping tale.

When I am done, I plan to place the book in the permanent collection of the Supreme Court Library, so that others will have an opportunity to read it.

Congratulations on the enormous effort the book represents (and, of course, on your work decades ago in the events it recounts).

Thank you for your many contributions to the Indiana bench and bar.

Sincerely,

Randy Shepard

Randall T. Shepard
Chief Justice of Indiana

3

In memory of Susanna Ellen

AUTHORS NOTE

The facts set forth in these materials are based upon actual facts. They are taken from trial documents, the official trial transcript, interviews with the persons directly concerned including investigating officers, jurors and attorneys, research and my memory. I have simplified or modified some of the materials but the basic facts are accurate. I have changed the names of the victims, and some non police witnesses to provide privacy.

This is the tragic story of William, Elizabeth Ann and Jenny Harold who were brutally murdered in the early morning of January 20, 1974, and of the trial of the accused, David James Roberts. Interwoven are important legal and constitutional issues.

This is also my story as a young man, student, lawyer and judge. I was the judge for the Roberts trial and it was the first murder trial involving the death penalty over which I presided.

I have included Notes at the end of the book which set forth additional or tangential materials which the reader may find interesting and informative.

Follow the criminal proceedings, read the trial evidence as it unfolds, assume you were on the jury, and decide the guilt or innocence of David James Roberts. Will you agree with the jury decision? Prepare for some surprises along the way.

John R. Berger
Angola, Indiana
January 1, 2016

STEUBEN COUNTY COURTHOUSE AND CIVIL WAR MONUMENT
Angola, Indiana

JOHN R. BERGER
Judge, Steuben Circuit Court
January 1, 1971

"Whoever intentionally takes the life of another with malice aforethought shall be guilty of the crime of murder."

The definition of murder under English common law.

PROLOGUE

New Whiteland, Indiana

It was about 4:30 a.m. on a cold and dark Sunday morning, January 20, 1974, in New Whiteland, a small middle class white residential community located in Johnson County fourteen miles south of Indianapolis, Indiana, when a passing car noticed smoke arising from the small suburban ranch home of William and Elizabeth Ann Harold located on 915 Pine Drive. Within five minutes the local volunteer fire department had arrived.

Upon entering the front door, the firefighters were met by a surge of fire coming from the middle section of the house. The house was fairly airtight and therefore the fire had not spread to the front and was mostly contained to a small den or TV room in the middle of the house. In ten minutes the fire was brought under control and extinguished.

When the firefighters first arrived they observed through a back bedroom window a baby bed. They broke the window, entered the bedroom and found the Harold's one year old daughter, Jenny, in her small bed still alive but unconscious. She died on the way to the hospital from smoke inhalation. Her first birthday was three days before.

The firefighters then searched the rest of the house. In the small den the burned bodies of William and Elizabeth Ann were found. They were 25 and 23 years of age.

Fortunately, their four year old daughter, Marie, was spending the night with her uncle.

The Investigation

The state fire marshal's office, state and local police thoroughly examined the Harold home for evidence as to the cause of the fire and the perpetrator of the crimes.

There was no evidence of forced entry. The front door was open when firefighters and police arrived. It was determined that the fire was caused by gasoline igniting. A red five gallon gas can was found in the den.

No evidence, other than the red gas can, was found at the house to indicate who committed these crimes.

Harold family members described the Harolds as a loving young couple who had been high school sweethearts. They were married shortly after graduation from high school. They were wonderful parents. They had two daughters, Jenny and Marie.

The neighborhood was canvassed by the police and forty-one neighbors were interviewed. No one had seen any visitors, salesmen or delivery persons in the afternoon or evening of the murders.

Investigators canvassed all service stations within the New Whiteland and Indianapolis areas to determine if possible the source of the red five gallon gas can.

Investigators determined from several witnesses that on the late afternoon prior to the murders at about 5:30 p.m. at a gas station at the corner of 16th and Meridian Streets in Indianapolis a black male in his late 20s, driving a 1970 tan or gold Buick Riviera, borrowed a five gallon red gas can with "$5 DEPOSIT ON THIS CAN" in yellow crayon on the side and had it filled with gasoline. One of the black employees stated to the investigator that he was the one who had sold the gas and delivered the gas can. It was the same gas can found at the scene of the murders.

After further thorough investigation, preliminary murder charges were filed and an arrest warrant issued for David James Roberts. Roberts was arrested and held without bail.

David James Roberts

When arrested Roberts lived in Indianapolis. He was African-American. He was 29 years old, 6'3'' tall, 195 lbs., had a light brown complexion, black hair, brown eyes, mustache and slight afro haircut. He had a tattoo "Carlos". He appeared to be well educated and was very articulate. He was attractive in appearance.

David James Roberts was born in Englewood, New Jersey, on January 25, 1944, and lived there for four years. His parents were African-American.

14

He had three brothers and three sisters ages 19-37. He had a deceased father and sister. His mother, sisters and brothers all lived in the Chicago, Illinois, area.

He attended grade school in Boston, Massachusetts and in New York State and attended high school in St. Paul, Minnesota. He did not have any attendance problems and got along well with his teachers.

He moved to the Chicago area in 1960. His father was self employed in the trucking business transporting frozen foods. He owned trucks and heavy equipment. He was very successful in this business until in the early 1950s when he developed diabetes and was unable to drive a truck or heavy equipment. Roberts worked with his father in Chicago until his father died in 1965 and the business was dissolved.

Roberts later moved to Indianapolis and attended Indiana-Purdue University in Indianapolis for three years. He enjoyed his college courses and received good grades.

In 1972 Roberts married Maryanne Duly. They had one child, Christopher, age 2. Roberts classified his marriage as a good one.

Roberts had worked in a steel mill and as a quality control inspector for Detroit Diesel in Indianapolis. He had speaking engagements at educational institutions in regard to penal reform. Roberts enjoyed fishing and reading all types of books, especially law and literature.

Roberts was born a Catholic and has attended church in the past. He stated that he believed in God.

Later the Johnson County Grand Jury issued Indictments for murder and arson against Roberts. He was formally arrested again and after several preliminary hearings before the judge of the Johnson Circuit Court, the case of State of Indiana v. David James Roberts was transferred for trial to the Steuben Circuit Court, Angola, Steuben County, Indiana. I was the Circuit Court judge and the case would be tried before me and heard by a Steuben County jury.

DAVID JAMES ROBERTS

PART ONE

STEUBEN COUNTY AND THE CIRCUIT COURT

CHAPTER ONE

Steuben County, Indiana
September 29, 1974

Steuben County is located in the far northeastern corner of Indiana. The history of Indiana[1] and its settlement were important ingredients in the selection of Steuben County as the Roberts trial venue.

Indiana was first settled in the southern part of the state by people of southern origin using water routes, primarily the Ohio River. They came from Virginia, Kentucky, North Carolina, Tennessee and Maryland. They brought with them their southern white heritage and opinions concerning African-Americans. By 1850 most settlers lived in the south half of Indiana. Beginning in about 1830, settlers from Ohio, Pennsylvania, New York and other northeastern states began to immigrate into the northeastern part of Indiana including Steuben County. Their heritage was northern with little prior contact with African-Americans. In the first quarter of the 1800s there were few settlers in the northern part and many Miami Indians. The Miami by treaty were removed to the Kansas Territory by 1846.

The first permanent settler in Steuben County was Gideon Langdon who built his log cabin in Jackson Township in 1831. Shortly thereafter other settlers began coming to Steuben County, primarily as part of the western migration of English Protestants from eastern states and New England. Early settlements included Jackson Prairie, Vermont Settlement and Nipcondish (Pleasant Lake). Steuben County was created in 1837 and named for Baron Frederick von Steuben, a Continental officer in the Revolutionary War.

At the time of the trial, Steuben County had a population of about 26,000. There was one city, Angola[2], with a population of about 5,000 and a beautiful 1917 Civil War Memorial Monument located in a large circle park in the center of the city. The monument is 85 feet tall and honored the 1,278 soldiers from Steuben County that served in the war of whom 280 never came home. Angola had no stop lights.

19

There were also several small towns in Steuben County. The county had a small industrial and commercial base, a large farm population, a small college, 101 beautiful glacier lakes which provided many recreational opportunities, and beautiful Pokagon State Park and Potawatomi Inn.

There was only one black family residing in Steuben County. The county had a scenic small lake called Fox Lake with all African-American summer residents. They were mostly professionals from the Toledo area. They were warmly accepted by the community and were about the only African-Americans with whom Steuben County residents had become acquainted.

From this mix of merchants, a small group of professionals, farmers, blue collar small factory workers, public school teachers, and college professors and employees a jury would be selected. As would be expected, the jury as finally selected did not have any African-American members. Even though there were not any African-Americans in the jury pool, because of the northern heritage of most Steuben County residents and their limited exposure to African-Americans, prosecution and defense counsel thought that they could select a jury that was not biased against African-Americans. Steuben County was a compromise as defense counsel wanted the case venued to an urban area and the prosecutor would not agree.

CHAPTER TWO

Steuben County Courthouse

Shortly after the Civil War, in 1867-1868, Freeborn Patterson designed and built the present brick courthouse in Angola for Steuben County.

He built it in the style of Faneuil Hall in Boston, a building famous for its role as a meeting place for patriots during the American Revolution. The court house is distinctive for its arched windows set in tall sunken panels, for its raking cornice carried by pairs of brackets, and for its curved wooden staircase. The construction cost was $26,392.00.

The courthouse was built on mostly donated land at the southeast corner of the public circle and its high cupola can be seen for many miles. The courthouse was enlarged in 1937 by adding to the south side at a cost of about $31,000.00. The courthouse was two stories high with a rustic basement. The first floor contained the offices of the County Clerk of Court, County Recorder, County Assessor and County Treasurer. The basement contained retired files and the Goodale Abstract Office.

The large circuit courtroom with a high ceiling and large arched windows, the judge's chambers, the court reporter's and bailiff's offices, and the probation officer's office occupied the entire second floor. Access was by means of two large beautiful wood staircases, one on each side of the entrance hall.

Originally there was a balcony overlooking the courtroom which was accessed by a small rickety winding staircase. The balcony had been closed and walled off for many years and was used as a storage area for old furniture and miscellaneous retired court files.

When I was judge there was no courthouse security as there is today. A few years ago someone in Oklahoma who was involved in a divorce action was not completely pleased with the judge's decision and shot His Honor dead in the courtroom. Immediately every courthouse in the nation had to have armed security. Not to be left behind, the Steuben County Commissioners since then have provided funds for two deputy sheriffs Monday through Friday from 7:30 a.m. until 5 p.m. to man the courthouse door, complete with walk through and hand held wand sensors.[3]

21

A cost comparison analysis would indicate that it would be a lot cheaper to not have security and lose a judge now and then.

On the wall of a hallway outside the court room hung a photograph of a 1918 all male jury that had deliberated the fate of Nora Coleman, a woman accused of murdering her mother. Old records of the case were found which included the Coroner's Report and an Affidavit by the defendant's husband.

The Coroner's Report stated that the deceased "had succumbed to her death from being shot in the head." It stated the cause of death as follows: "I find that the deceased came to her death as the result of being shot in the head with gun shot charge entering just above right ear and lodging in the skull." These were the complete findings of cause of death. It is interesting to compare this report to the detailed many paged coroner's reports of modern times. In 1918 they did not elaborate on the obvious.

The Affidavit of the husband stated, "I, Word Coleman, being duly sworn make statement as follows:

About 4 o'clock a.m., Feb 7, 1918, my wife awoke me at which time she fixed fires and came to bed.

She said to me that I would not need to be bothered with mother any more for she had took the gun up there and shot her.

When I asked her why she did it she said so she would not keep harrissing (sic) me. She gave no other reason."

She was a good wife. She kept the house warm and took care of a bothersome mother-in-law.

CHAPTER THREE

The Judge

A trial judge's legal training, prior law practice and judicial experience are very important in formulating a judge's thoughts and decisions. However, a judge's background, life experiences including military service and being a husband and father, compassion, courtesy, and an ability to keep an open mind without bias are vital components in a judge's decisions.

I was born to loving parents in Cincinnati, Ohio, on January 11, 1929. I had an older sister and brother, Peggy and George. I was named John after my father and great grandfather. We lived in a small house on one of the hills overlooking downtown Cincinnati.[4]

I attended Sacred Heart Academy for my first year of school. The only remembrance I have of first grade is standing on the stage for our recital with Sister Marie conducting and proud parents in attendance. At the appropriate time we all bowed down to avoid hitting our heads on the bridge as we sang the chorus of *Fifteen Miles on the Erie Canal.*

> Low bridge, ev'rybody down,
> Low bridge 'cause we're com-in to a town,
> And you'll always know your neighbor,
> You'll always know your pal,
> If you've ever navigated on the Erie Canal.

I was the only boy in the class. I wonder if this had any deep psychological effect on my later life and opinion of women.

I transferred for the rest of grade school to Annunciation Catholic School, a converted church building with four classrooms near my home. Two grades were in each room presided over by a stern and loving Franciscan Sister. Father Kelly was the pastor of the adjoining church and each Monday morning quizzed the faithful children on their knowledge of the *Catechism*. They had spent many hours each week memorizing the answers to the questions contained therein. I still remember the first question and answer: Question: "Who made you?" Correct answer: "God made me."

In the seventh grade I was introduced by my parents to the adult world. They gave me a copy of *Sane Sex Life and Sane Safe Living*. I was told to only read the third chapter and not look at any of the graphic diagrams or photographs in other chapters! This was the extent of my formal sex education. I guess I did not read the third chapter very well. When asked by a ninth grader if I knew what a fisherman's dream was, and after I answered "No", he replied "Two nights on Veronica Lake." I asked where Veronica Lake was located.

When my daughter was in the sixth grade the world had changed. No longer were parents responsible for sex education. Our school board, after heated discussions, decided four to three to require all sixth grade students to have a two hour session (together with a graphic slide presentation of the male and female reproductive organs and sperm valiantly seeking their goal like Alaskan salmon in a Kenai stream) to inform the maturing students concerning the intricacies of reproduction. Mrs. Belair, a retired second grade teacher, was selected to give the session because of her known expertise in this area. My wife and daughter attended one of the first sessions. After the session, upon returning to our home, my wife sat down quietly with our daughter and asked lovingly if she had any questions. Our daughter replied, "Mom, I didn't understand anything."

Three years of high school then followed at Cincinnati Country Day School, a private school for boys, grades 1-12. There were twelve students in my junior year class and there were no seniors. The classes were rigorous and included Latin, French, Spanish, grammar and the classics.

When I think of grammar, I always remember my dear grandmother Lester from Tuscaloosa, Alabama, who had a reverence for grammar. She said it was what separated one from the "common folks." She often reminded me that there are four very important things to remember: Corn is raised and people are reared, Horses sweat and people perspire, Meals are prepared and animals are fixed, and People become angry and dogs become mad.

I had a normal high school social life with only one caveat. My mother had a southern lady background and required me, as an aspiring gentleman, to attempt to learn ballroom dancing. I was duly enrolled in Madame Fedarova's dance classes which met monthly at a grand ballroom

24

at the Vernon Manor Hotel. There I met the daughters of Cincinnati society, one of whom I am sure my mother intended me to someday wed. I disappointed her.

I attended law school at an Ivy League school. My first introduction to the Ivy League was at my brother's bachelor's dinner the night before his wedding. I was seventeen, about to enter college, and a man!

My brother was twenty three. He had received a medical discharge from the Army after being wounded near the Arno River in Italy while serving in the U.S. Fifth Army under General Mark Clark in the second war to end all wars. He was a front line medic when the average life expectancy of a medic was measured in days. The home front tried to keep their spirits up by listening to Vaughn Monroe singing "When the lights go on again all over the world" (Then we'll have time for things like wedding rings and free hearts will sing) and Kay Kyser's "Praise the Lord and pass the ammunition" (and we'll all stay free).

My brother was about to marry his sweetheart, a delightful young lady from a traditional Yale family. The dinner was of course at Mory's in New Haven, the iconic private membership "Yalie" eating club founded in 1849. The dinner was celebrated in the large and very impressive upper room of Mory's. Throughout dinner a very large loving cup filled with champagne was passed between the revelers and we each took a large sip. There were many toasts. A final toast was given at the end of the dinner and we all thrust our wine glasses into the burning fireplace where they shattered in a beautiful array of reflected colors. We then stood, and solemnly bid good wishes to my brother by singing *The Whiffenpoof Song*:

To the tables down at Mory's,

To the place where Louis dwells,

To the dear old Temple Bar

We love so well,

Sing the Whiffenpoofs assembled

With their glasses raised on high,

And the magic of their singing casts its spell.

We are poor little lambs

25

Who have lost our way.

Baa! Baa! Baa!

We are little black sheep

Who have gone astray.

Baa! Baa! Baa!

After my junior year in high school, the WWII draft was still in full swing. I was seventeen. In order to attend college before being drafted, I enrolled after my junior year in high school at Hillsdale College, a small liberal arts college in Hillsdale, Michigan, under a wartime early enrollment program. I was teased later in life for practicing law when I did not even have a high school diploma.

I majored in physics at Hillsdale and was deferred from the draft and Korea.[5]

Upon graduation, I received the University of Michigan Horace Rackham Graduate School of Science scholarship for two years of graduate study in physics. The scholarship was tempting but prompted by excellent courses in constitutional history and business law at Hillsdale College, I decided to become a lawyer. I did not accept the scholarship to the great surprise and joy of the alternate, and to the chagrin of my father who would now have to pay tuition, room and board.

Thus started my legal pursuit. I applied to only one law school, Harvard Law School.

I was accepted and in early September of 1950, with some trepidation, at the age of twenty-one headed east on US Highway 20 in my new bright red 1950 Ford convertible (a graduation present from my parents) toward Cambridge, Massachusetts, and to the unknown.

Law school consisted of three years of concentrated studies including the core courses of criminal law, torts, contracts, property law, domestic relations, commercial transactions, civil law and procedure, administrative law, constitutional law, taxation and jurisprudence. The 1950-1951 first year law class consisted of about five hundred students including for the first time twelve women. Classes were held six days a week. Classes were divided into four sections of 125 students. Each section attended class together in 150 seat stadium type classrooms. This was a new experience for me as I had twelve students in each class at Cincinnati Country Day School and usually twenty at Hillsdale College.

While at law school I took a tour of Faneuil Hall located in adjoining Boston, never dreaming that one day I would be a judge presiding in a courthouse that was an exact replica.

After three years of rigorous study, I was graduated from Harvard Law School with a Doctor of Jurisprudence degree in 1953.[6]

During the summer of 1953, I took and passed the two day Indiana bar examination and was admitted to the Indiana and Federal bar in November of 1953.[7]

The Korean War was still ongoing in the summer of 1953 and I was drafted into the Army as a Private at the age of twenty-four.[8]

Since I had an undergraduate degree in physics and a Doctorate of Law degree, the Army decided that I should be taught to assemble bridges and would make a perfect Field Engineer. I was assigned to Fort Leonard Wood, Missouri, for sixteen weeks of basic and advanced training.[9] An armistice had been signed at Panmunjom on July 27, 1953 which effectively ended the fighting and, after basic, I was assigned as a field radio repair instructor at Fort Monmouth, New Jersey for the remainder of my two year active duty requirement. The armistice still stands and, because South Korea never has agreed to the armistice, South Korea and North Korea are still technically at war. I am very thankful that, because of the armistice, I was not sent to the front lines of Korea. After active duty I was required to be in the Ready Army Reserve for six additional years during which period I was subject to active duty call up upon 24 hour notice. I was almost called up for service during the Berlin Airlift. I received an Honorable Discharge from the Army in December, 1961. I am very proud to have served my country.

The Berger family had spent summers at Lake James in Steuben County since 1936 and in 1946 my parents moved permanently to adjoining Jimmerson Lake. After release from Army active duty I lived with them until my marriage in 1962 to Susanna Ellen Lemley, an attractive and vivacious Angola first grade teacher. Susanna and I built a home near my parents on Jimmerson Lake. Susanna and I have two children, Susan Elizabeth (1966) and John Christopher (1969).

I decided to start my law career in the small community of Angola rather than in a metropolitan area. I have never regretted this decision.

27

In January of 1956, at the age of twenty-six, I joined two local attorneys, Donald Trennepohl, a graduate of Indiana Law School, and Wilson Shoup, a graduate of Georgetown University Law School, to form the legal partnership of Trennepohl, Berger & Shoup (we flipped a coin to determine the name sequence). The partnership continued for 15 years until I was elected judge of the Steuben Circuit Court.[10]

My election for judge of the Steuben Circuit Court was hotly contested. Indiana circuit court judges are elected on a partisan basis with a primary and general election.

Up until 1970, no doubt by virtue of the traditional egalitarian view, Indiana circuit judges were not required to be lawyers and admitted to the bar. In 1970, Article VII of the 1851 Indiana Constitution was amended to provide that all circuit court judges "shall have been duly admitted to practice law by the Supreme Court of Indiana."

I had to first run in the Republican primary against Olin Dygert, a friendly, fatherly and well respected local Steuben County constitutional lawyer. I won the primary by 87 votes.

In the general election I ran against the incumbent democrat judge, Judge Louis Sisler, who had been appointed by a democrat governor two years before to fill a vacancy. The vacancy was created when the Steuben Circuit judge, Roger DeBruler, was appointed to the Indiana Supreme Court in September of 1968.

Running against the incumbent is never an easy task. Further problems with my campaign arose because I was perceived by some as an outsider (not having been born in Steuben County) and because others were not sure that a Harvard graduate would be able to relate to the common man. I ran a vigorous campaign. I sent out three thousand letters and posted signs on about every telephone pole in Steuben County. I went to almost every farm house (sometimes a barn or milking shed) in the county asking for votes. I went to many pot lucks and gave brief presentations as to my many abilities. At one potluck in the basement of the R.E.M.C. an aspiring J. Danforth Quayle, later to be Vice-President, was present and making his pitch to be elected to Congress. His assistant at the potluck was Dan Coats, later to be a Senator and Ambassador to Germany

I won by a narrow margin.[11] Both Dans went on to worldly challenges and I stayed home to serve my community. I am reminded of one of my favorite poems, *The Vision of Sir Launfal*, by James Russell Lowell:

28

The little bird sits at his door in the sun,

Atilt like a blossom among the leaves,

And lets his illuminated being o'errun

With the deluge of summer it receives;

His mate feels the eggs beneath her wings,

And the heart in her dumb breast flutters and sings;

He sings to the wide world, and she to her nest,-

In the nice ear of Nature, which song is the best?

On January 1, 1971, in the old high ceiling county courtroom, I was sworn in as judge of the Steuben Circuit Court by the clerk of court before a small group of friends, court personnel and my loving wife and two small children. The elderly bailiff, Russell Jackson, and court reporter, Iona Crain, presented me with a beautiful walnut engraved gavel which I cherish to this day.

CHAPTER FOUR

The Circuit Court

Each of the 92 counties in Indiana is served by a Circuit Court.

Originally, several counties were served by a single judge who presided over the courts of all counties in the circuit. He would go "on circuit" and thus the name circuit judge. The first crcuit court that served Steuben County was established in 1839. Originally Steuben County and DeKalb County to the south were served by one circuit judge. Then Steuben County and LaGrange County to the west were served by one circuit judge. This was the situation until about 1950 when Steuben and LaGrange were separated and each had its own circuit court judge.

When I became judge, the court system in Steuben County consisted of the Steuben Circuit Court and two lower courts, a Justice of the Peace Court in the Town of Fremont and an Angola City Court, both of which had jurisdiction limited to traffic violations and small claims. Upon request by either party, a decision of these courts could be appealed and tried de-novo in the Steuben Circuit Court.

The circuit court had unlimited general jurisdiction of all matters and was the basic trial court in Indiana.

There were five divisions of the circuit court consisting of criminal, civil, juvenile, domestic relations (divorce) and probate (wills, trusts and the administration thereof). All divisions were interchangeable and administered at the same time by the judge of the Steuben Circuit Court.[12]

There was only one judge and I was the judge. My court personnel consisted of a Court Reporter, Iona Crain, who reported all evidence, testimony and court actions by shorthand or on an old tape recorder, a Bailiff, Russell Jackson, who acted as a receptionist and was in charge of the court room and juries, and a Probation Officer who usually was a minister and was part time. I immediately elevated the probation office to full time and appointed Thomas Hanselman, a former Steuben County Sheriff, as Probation Officer.

Judgments of the circuit court could be appealed to the Indiana Court of Appeals or in appropriate matters, to the Indiana Supreme Court. All murder convictions, sentences and judgments were appealed directly to the Indiana Supreme Court.

Many people think that if an accused is found guilty that he or she can appeal to a "higher court" and get a new trial before an appellate court. This concept is wrong. A defendant gets only one chance to have a trial and that is before the circuit court.

An appellate court cannot substitute its opinion of the facts for that of the jury and trial court. No new evidence is presented before an appellate court. The appellate court will only review the evidence presented at the trial court. The appellate court will review whether the trial court evidence favorable to the State is sufficient to sustain a verdict of guilty and only if it does not, will it reverse the conviction. Rarely is a verdict reversed on this basis.

The appellate court primarily rules on errors of law that the trial judge may have made. Examples of errors of law are an improper jury instruction given by the judge, or the judge allowing improper evidence or testimony over proper objection to be introduced by counsel. The Appellate Court must find a serious and prejudicial error of law made by the trial judge in order to reverse a guilty verdict.

Therefore, David James Roberts realistically would get only one chance to defend himself against the charges brought against him. He would have to seek a not guilty verdict from the Steuben Circuit Court jury.

PART TWO

THE TRIAL

CHAPTER FIVE

The Grand Jury
Johnson Circuit Court
March 15, 1974

Indiana law provided that a felony criminal charge could be commenced in two ways. The prosecuting attorney of the county where the crime occurred could file a charging Information setting forth the crime and the person charged, or a grand jury could issue an Indictment setting forth the crime and the person charged. Both would be filed in the circuit court of the county where the crime occurred.

A grand jury in Indiana consists of six members. It is convened by the circuit judge either by the judge deciding to convene a grand jury or at the request of the prosecuting attorney. The grand jury in secret hears and examines evidence presented by the prosecuting attorney concerning crimes to determine whether an Indictment should issue charging a defendant (called a Target under present Indiana law) with a crime. If an Indictment is issued it is called "A True Bill." If the grand jury decides that an Indictment should not be issued it is "Not a True Bill", which was originally called an "Ignoramus" (We know of no facts) in England.

Even though the jurors have the right to call witnesses, in practice the prosecutor decides which crimes to present and which witnesses to call. In this way, the prosecutor may shape the proceedings to almost ensure an Indictment being issued or to suggest that the grand jury decline to indict. The proceedings are usually ex parte and the defendant has no knowledge thereof. Any member of the grand jury also has the right to request his fellow jurors to commence an investigation as to any offense.

A grand jury in issuing an Indictment does not determine the guilt of a defendant. It merely finds that from the evidence presented to them that the defendant probably committed the crime. An Indictment and an Information are merely methods to officially charge a defendant with a crime. Whether the defendant is guilty (beyond a reasonable doubt) will be up to a judge or jury. At trial, the jury is instructed by the judge that the filing of an Information or Indictment is no evidence of guilt.

When I was judge a grand jury was required by law to annually examine the condition and management of all county, city and town jails and file a written report with the judge. The inmates always knew when the grand jury was in session as the meals were measurably better.

Often the grand jury option is used by a prosecuting attorney when the prosecutor does not want the sole responsibility for charges being filed or not being filed. This usually occurs when the facts present a circumstantial case or may have racial overtones as in the Roberts case.

The Roberts case was commenced by Grand Jury Indictment.

All federal prosecutions for felonies can only be commenced by grand jury indictment (16 to 23 members) pursuant to the Fifth Amendment. The Founding Fathers wanted to protect the people from arbitrary authority of the government to commence a criminal prosecution. The grand jury would represent the people and protect their interests. Charges could not be brought unless the people sitting on a grand jury decided that charges should be brought. This Fifth Amendment grand jury requirement is not binding upon the states.

Indiana in the 1816 Constitution adopted the requirement of a grand jury for felony prosecutions based upon the same theory to protect the people from arbitrary government action. However, grand juries were increasingly commencing investigations on their own and imposing their views as to proper public order and public virtue, and issuing Indictments based thereon. Their deliberations were in secret and ex parte. As a result of this practice and the rise of Jacksonian individualism, there was great pressure to repeal the Constitutional grand jury requirement. All things done in private were suspect. A compromise was agreed upon and the new 1851 Indiana Constitution provided that the grand jury procedure would remain but that the legislature could provide additional methods to commence a criminal prosecution. The legislature did so and provided that a criminal prosecution could also be brought by the prosecuting attorney by Information. The traditional right of a grand jury to investigate crimes and file Indictments on their own was abrogated by the Indiana legislature in 1981. Henceforth, no Indictment could be filed with the court unless the prosecuting attorney approved.

Traditionally there were two types of first degree murder. The first type was intentionally taking the life of another person with premeditation and malice. The second was taking the life

36

of another person which resulted from the commission of a felony (a serious crime). Intent to kill, malice and premeditation was not required. This is called "felony murder."

Since the crimes were committed in Johnson County, the facts and circumstances of the crimes were submitted to a six member Johnson Circuit Court grand jury. After hearing the evidence presented by Joe Van Valer, prosecuting attorney of Johnson County, Indiana, the county where New Whiteland is located, the grand jury issued its unanimous Indictment against David James Roberts in six counts:

Count I: Murder in the First Degree by intentionally taking the life of William Harold with premeditation and malice;

Count II: Murder in the First Degree by taking the life of William Harold while in the commission of burglary; (felony murder)

Count III: Murder in the First Degree by intentionally taking the life of Elizabeth Ann Harold with premeditation and malice;

Count IV: Murder in the First Degree by taking the life of Elizabeth Ann Harold while in the commission of burglary; (felony murder)

Count V: Murder in the First Degree by taking the life of Jenny Lynn Harold while in the commission of Arson; (felony murder) and

Count VI: committing First Degree Arson by willfully and maliciously burning a dwelling house.

Under Indiana law at that time Counts I, II, III, IV and V were punishable by life imprisonment. If however Counts II, IV or V were committed by a person with a prior unrelated conviction of robbery, then the penalty was death. Count VI was punishable by an indeterminate sentence of five to twenty years, the exact length to be determined by the Indiana Department of Corrections.

The six count Indictment was filed in the Johnson Circuit Court in Franklin, Indiana, and approved by the prosecuting attorney and judge. The judge issued a formal arrest warrant for David James Roberts to be held without bail which was served upon Roberts. Roberts was already being held on preliminary charges in the Johnson County jail.

37

CHAPTER SIX

Preliminary Hearing
Johnson Circuit Court
March 26, 1974

On March 26, 1974, Roberts, shackled and in the custody of two deputy sheriffs, appeared before Judge Robert Young of the Johnson Circuit Court in Franklin, Indiana, for a preliminary hearing. Joe Van Valer, prosecuting attorney, was present. There were only three other persons in the courtroom. Two appeared to be curious attorneys and one appeared to be a reporter.

Roberts was advised of the charges against him, the possible penalties, and his constitutional rights including the right to be represented by an attorney at no expense to him if he could not afford to employ an attorney.

Roberts asked that an attorney be appointed for him and the judge, after an examination of his assets and income, determined that Roberts did not have assets or income available to him to afford engaging private counsel and that pauper counsel should be appointed. The judge then appointed Tom Jones, a Franklin defense attorney, to represent Roberts.

The judge then told Roberts that the matter would be set for formal arraignment after he had a chance to confer with his attorney. At the arraignment Roberts would be again advised of his constitutional rights and asked to enter his plea-guilty or not guilty.

Roberts then stood up and asked if he could address the court. The judge gave him permission.

"Your Honor, a terrible mistake has been made in charging me with any crime. I am innocent. There cannot possibly be any evidence implicating me in these horrible crimes. Please release me without posting bond on my personal recognizance. Let me return to my family and job."

The judge wondered where Roberts had learned the term "personal recognizance" (it was a legal term that meant his personal promise to return to court when asked).

38

The judge patiently explained to Roberts that the court could not release him. With a charge of murder the law required that he be held without bail. He should talk to his attorney, Tom Jones, before he discussed this matter with anyone.

Judge Young then remanded Roberts to the custody of the Johnson County Sheriff to be held without bail.

The prosecutor, Joe Van Valer and defense counsel, Tom Jones, were in their 30s, experienced in criminal cases, well educated, intelligent and always well prepared.

Tom Jones had never served as defense counsel in a case where the death sentence was involved. Under present Indiana Criminal Trial Rules, he would not have been qualified to serve as defense attorney for Roberts. Now, when a death sentence is sought, the judge must appoint two attorneys to represent the defendant, a lead counsel and co-counsel. They must have at least five and three years criminal litigation experience, five and three years felony jury trial experience, one attorney must have been counsel in at least one case in which the death penalty was sought, and both must have completed at least twelve hours of special training in defense of capital cases within the previous two years.

CHAPTER SEVEN
Bail Hearing
Johnson Circuit Court
September 16, 1974

Even though the Eighth Amendment to the U.S. Constitution prohibits excessive bail, this prohibition has been interpreted not to require bail when the charge is murder. The Indiana Constitution provides that there shall be no bail for murder "where the proof is evident, or the presumption strong." This concept was incorporated in the original 1816 Indiana Constitution and reaffirmed in the 1851 Constitution.

Therefore under Indiana law, if a defendant was being held in prison on a charge of murder no bail was available unless the proof of guilt was not evident or the presumption of guilt was not strong. A defendant could challenge his imprisonment without bail by filing a Petition for Writ of Habeas Corpus and To Be Let to Bail with the circuit court asking for an evidentiary hearing.

At such a hearing under the Indiana practice at that time, the defendant had the burden of proving that the evidence of guilt against him was not evident nor the presumption of guilt strong. If a defendant can sustain this burden, the court must set a reasonable bail amount and upon posting sufficient bond, the defendant must be released from custody. This practice was codified as of 1981. So much for the presumption of innocence. How does a defendant prove that his guilt is not evident or the presumption of guilt is not strong? Does the defendant have to call the state's witnesses and ask them "What evidence do you have against me?"

On June 25, 2013, the Indiana Supreme Court in a 3-2 decision (Fry v. State of Indiana) decided wisely that placing the burden of proof upon the defendant was unconstitutional and that henceforth the burden would be upon the prosecuting attorney to prove that the evidence of guilt was evident or that the presumption of guilt was strong. The proof must be by a preponderance of the evidence (more likely than not).

Often an experienced criminal defense attorney would file such a petition to be able to find out what evidence the prosecutor had against the defendant with no real expectation of being able to obtain release of the defendant from jail on bail.

Roberts through his attorney, Tom Jones, filed such a petition and a hearing date before the Johnson Circuit Court was set. Tom Jones did not expect to be able to obtain bail for Roberts but took advantage of the procedure to obtain what amounted to a free deposition, an examination under oath, of the prosecutor's witnesses. Roberts surprisingly was confident that the judge would set bail and allow him to post bond and be released.

The hearing was held September 16, 1974. David James Roberts, Joe Van Valer, prosecuting attorney, and Tom Jones, defense counsel, were present at the hearing before Judge Robert Young.

At the hearing testimony was presented as to the evidence found at the Harold residence including the fact that a red five gallon gas can was found in the den.

Richard Roman, an employee of Renkite Shell Station, Indianapolis, was then called upon to testify concerning a red gas can and gas purchase. He testified that he had in fact sold gas and delivered a red five gallon gas can to a black male in his late twenties at about 5:30 p.m. on the afternoon before the murders.

He was then asked if he could identify and, if so, point to the person who had purchased the gas and received the gas can. Richard Roman nervously looked around the courtroom and directly at Roberts. Richard hesitated and then stated to the judge that he did not see anyone in the courtroom who looked like the gas purchaser or the person who received the gas can.

The prosecutor, Joe Van Valer, was stunned as the police had told him that Richard Roman had previously told the police that Roberts was that person.

William Hardy was the next witness to testify. He was another gas station employee at Renkite Shell and was a witness to the gas purchase and can delivery. He also had previously told the police that Roberts was that person. He was asked if he could identify Roberts as the person who had received the gas can. William Hardy gave the same response as Richard Roman. Neither identified Roberts!

Judge Young asked the prosecutor if he had any further evidence to introduce. The prosecutor did not offer any further evidence and Judge Young thereupon found that the evidence of guilt

41

was not clear and convincing, that Roberts did not pose an eminent risk of flight to avoid prosecution, and set bail at $10,000.00.

Roberts was not surprised. He had said all along that they had the wrong man. Tom Jones told Roberts that he would meet with Joe Van Valer and discuss a dismissal. The prosecution obviously had no case.

Roberts immediately posted a $10,000.00 bond and was released from custody.

The prosecutor would not dismiss the case. The prosecutor was up for election in November in a hotly contested prosecutor's race. How would it look to the Johnson County voters if the prosecutor dismissed triple murder charges approved by six honorable Johnson County grand jurors?

CHAPTER EIGHT

Change of Venue Hearing
Johnson Circuit Court
September 17, 1974

Indiana law provides that in a criminal matter a defendant can request a change of venue to transfer a case to another Indiana county. Such a transfer is discretionary with the trial judge and can be granted if the judge believes that the defendant cannot receive a fair jury trial in the county where the crime was committed because of prejudicial pretrial publicity.

The Harold murders and Roberts subsequent arrest received complete and repeated coverage in the Indianapolis newspapers, which were widely circulated in Johnson County, as well as the local Johnson County newspaper.

On September 17, 1974, one day after the bail hearing, Tom Jones filed a Motion to Change Venue from the County with the Johnson Circuit Court contending that such publicity was highly prejudicial to Roberts and that the defendant could not obtain a fair and impartial jury in Johnson County. At the hearing many newspaper articles were presented to the judge and the motion was granted.

It is not surprising that the change of venue was granted as the docket is always overwhelming in the circuit court of a non metropolitan county with only one judge. A two or three week jury trial would wreck havoc with the court calendar. Also, the case was certainly inflammatory and was the type of case that a judge does not hesitate to transfer.

Counsel were instructed by the judge to try and agree on an appropriate county to which the case would be transferred for further proceedings and trial and if they could not agree, the judge would name three counties from which the parties would alternately strike. Counsel agreed that a county far removed from the metropolitan Indianapolis area would be best.

After talking with several attorneys in Angola, the county seat of Steuben County, 120 miles northeast of Indianapolis, concerning the demographic of Steuben County and the competence and experience of the Steuben Circuit Court judge, counsel agreed that the case be transferred to the Steuben Circuit Court, Angola, Indiana, the Honorable John R. Berger presiding. Pursuant to the agreement, the case was so transferred.

I was the sole judge of the Steuben Circuit Court. I was first made aware of a criminal case being transferred to Steuben County when, during a coffee break at Bassett's Restaurant across the street from the courthouse, two local attorneys reported to me that they had been contacted by Franklin attorneys concerning the circuit judge and the community. The local attorneys said it was a high profile murder case with a black defendant. They wanted to know if I knew anything about it. I didn't.

I wondered why the defense agreed to transfer the trial of an African-American to Steuben County rather than to an urban area with a large African-American population. The jury in Steuben County would undoubtedly be all white. This concerned me very much.

Although a judge to whom a case will be transferred cannot refuse a transfer to the court, usually the transferring judge will contact the judge of the court where the case will be transferred and obtain consent. This was not done in the Roberts case, probably because Judge Young knew there would be reluctance to accept transfer if the facts of the case were known.

When the case file was received and filed in the Steuben Circuit Court on September 23, 1974, I knew that the case would be a tremendous challenge especially since the State was seeking the death penalty. *State of Indiana v. David James Roberts* was the only murder trial involving the death penalty over which I presided as judge. A search of the docket of the Steuben Circuit Court reveals that from its inception in 1839 until the present, except for the *Roberts* case, there has not been a murder case tried where the death sentence was requested.

I had no way of knowing the physical, mental and emotional strain that there would be upon me and my family.

CHAPTER NINE

Arraignment
Steuben Circuit Court
October 21, 1974

On October 21, 1974, David James Roberts, Joe Van Valer, the prosecuting attorney of Johnson County, and Tom Jones, defense counsel, appeared before me as judge of the Steuben Circuit Court in the old court house in Angola for formal arraignment.

Just before the arrival of Roberts and Jones, I was looking out the window of my second story chambers and noticed the arrival by car of two young men with brief cases dressed in suits with ties. I noted to the court reporter and bailiff that two of the attorneys in the Roberts case had arrived. It was only when the men appeared in court and after introductions that I realized that one of the men was the defendant, Roberts. Roberts' appearance, demeanor, intelligence and communication skills were well above average. He was always dressed in a suit and tie.

After the trial, one of the jurors told me that when the jurors were first present they wondered where the defendant was. At the defense table were defense counsel Tom Jones and David James Roberts. They thought that Roberts was another defense attorney!

When all were present in the courtroom, upon motion, I gave Craig Benson, the Steuben County prosecutor, permission to assist Joe Van Valer in the prosecution, and appointed Steuben County attorney Albert Friend as co-counsel for the defense to assist Tom Jones. Local co-counsel is especially helpful in the selection of local jurors. They also present a local presence which makes a venued cause more familiar and acceptable to the jury.

I then read to Roberts the Indictments and explained the statutes under which the Indictments were drawn including the possible penalties (life imprisonment and death).

I further explained in detail the defendant's constitutional rights including the right to be presented with witnesses against him before an impartial judge or jury, the right to call witnesses on his behalf, the right to a speedy trial, the right not to be compelled to be a witness against himself and the right to a jury trial before twelve jurors selected from Steuben County.

I also explained that a judge or jury must find the defendant guilty of a crime beyond a reasonable doubt before he can be convicted of any crime and if there is a jury trial, the jury must be unanimous in its decision before a conviction or acquittal. Roberts then told me that he fully understood the charges against him and his rights, entered a plea of "not guilty" to all charges and requested that all matters be tried by jury. The jury trial request was automatically granted and bail previously set by the Johnson Circuit Court was continued without objection.

I set the matter for an Omnibus Hearing.

CHAPTER TEN

Omnibus Hearing

Steuben Circuit Court

March 11, 1975

At an omnibus hearing the attorneys exchange the names and addresses of prospective witnesses with the substance of their testimony, and a list of proposed documentary and forensic evidence. Also, any motions are considered by the judge. At this time the requirement of an omnibus hearing was fairly new. Previously, the prosecutor and defense counsel did not know prior to trial what witnesses or other evidence would be introduced. This made it especially difficult to prepare a defense. We used to call it "trial by ambush."

Joe Van Valer had lost his bid in November for reelection as prosecutor of Johnson County. Charles Gantz, an accomplished Franklin attorney in his mid thirties had defeated Van Valer. In spite of the disastrous bail hearing, Charles Gantz had refused to dismiss the Roberts case and was preparing for trial. Mr. Gantz was convinced that Roberts was guilty.

The hearing was held March 11, 1975. At the hearing the newly elected prosecuting attorney of Johnson County, Charles Gantz, submitted a list of forty five prospective witnesses. Defense counsel, Tom Jones, submitted a list of eight. Defense counsel did not know at that time whether the defendant would be testifying.

I submitted for approval or objection twenty-three Preliminary Instructions which I would read to the jury at the commencement of the trial explaining the charges of murder, arson, burglary, the possible penalties, the presumption of innocence, the definition of malice and premeditation, and the fact that each juror must be convinced beyond a reasonable doubt as to the guilt of defendant before he could return a guilty verdict. The instructions were approved.

Both the prosecutor and defense counsel filed Motions in Limine. Such motions if granted would forbid counsel or any witness from mentioning certain facts at the trial.

Defense counsel had indicated that the defense had evidence that Buddy Harold, a prospective witness for the prosecution and the brother of William Harold, had embezzled funds as Executor of the Harold estates and as Guardian for the surviving Harold child, Marie, and that such evidence would be offered to impeach his testimony. Evidence that a witness is a thief can be considered by the jury as evidence that the witness is not truthful in his testimony. The prosecutor wanted any such evidence excluded unless, after a hearing out of the presence of the jury, I found any such evidence credible.

The defense filed motions to exclude any evidence or testimony of previous charges against Roberts. I will discuss these motions later.

I granted all motions.

The defendant also filed Notice of Alibi which stated that defendant intended to introduce evidence that he was in fact at the Fall Creek Y.M.C.A. the evening and morning of the murders.

Tom Jones requested that I authorize the employment of an arson cause and reconstruction expert at a cost of between $900.00 and $1200.00. I granted the request.

I spent considerable time preparing for the trial. Such preparation consisted mainly of anticipating what witnesses might testify and what objections might be made by counsel to proposed questions. Also possible objections to the introduction of any other evidence needed to be considered. If necessary the judge needed to research the law in advance of trial as to a proper ruling on any objections. In the heat of a fast paced murder trial the judge must be able to rule immediately (and correctly) on all objections. A judge cannot recess the trial to do research every time there is an objection. An incorrect ruling on the admission or exclusion of evidence could result in an appellate court reversal and new trial.

Also adding to the pressure upon the trial judge in a jurisdiction where there is only one judge, is the fact that the judge, in addition to presiding over the trial, must also be available to conduct other matters within the court's jurisdiction. The judge must conduct arraignments for new criminal cases, approve new criminal cases and order warrants to be issued, hold juvenile hearings, make emergency orders in divorce and custody matters, and hold temporary mental commitment hearings.

I also did considerable research in regard to recent United States Supreme Court decisions as to the death sentence and to the qualification of jurors in respect thereto.

The constitutionality of the death sentence per se had been presented to the United States Supreme Court many times. It had consistently been upheld. However, certain aspects of the imposition of the death sentence had also been considered.

The United States Supreme Court on June 29, 1972, three years before the Roberts trial, in *Furman v. Georgia* had decided that the Georgia and Texas criminal statutes allowing juries, after they had heard the evidence, to decide guilt and impose the death sentence without being given any guidelines as to under what circumstances they could impose the death sentence rather than a life imprisonment sentence was unconstitutional. Any such practice or law violated the Eighth Amendment which prohibited cruel and unusual punishments and was incorporated by the Fourteenth Amendment. Defendant Furman, an African-American, had been surprised by a homeowner during an attempted burglary. He tried to flee, tripped, fell and accidentally discharged his gun killing the homeowner. The jury had sentenced him to death.

Indiana's murder and death penalty criminal statutes, together with 39 other states statutes, were similar to Georgia's and therefore became unconstitutional by virtue of the Furman decision.

The Attorney General of Indiana, Theodore Sendak, had filed a brief amicus curiae (a friend of the court) with the Supreme Court in the Furman case urging that the Georgia and Texas statutes be upheld. This was Indiana taxpayers' money being spent on a lost cause.

On May 1, 1973, the Indiana Legislature, following the lead of many other state legislatures, quickly passed a new murder and death penalty statute which was intended to avoid the Furman case. The new Indiana law mandated the death sentence in certain circumstances (killing a human being while perpetrating or attempting to perpetrate arson or burglary by a person who has a prior unrelated felony conviction of robbery) and therefore, the legislature reasoned, guidelines were not necessary. The death sentence was mandatory and therefore a jury would have no discretion. No need to provide guidelines. Roberts would be tried under this new 1973 statute. If Roberts was found guilty by the jury of murder as charged, and if Roberts had a prior robbery conviction, the jury by law would have to sentence Roberts to death!

In anticipation of a large number of prospective jurors being challenged and excused at trial, I issued a venire to the sheriff of Steuben County to summon forty prospective jurors to appear for trial on July 1, 1975 at 8 a.m.

The jurors selected for a particular trial were chosen from a pool of prospective jurors selected by the Steuben County Jury Commissioners. The two Jury Commissioners are appointed by the Circuit Court judge. Their function at the time of the Roberts trial was to meet every three months to select a number of prospective jurors from a list of property owners in Steuben County. In the smaller counties, the jury commissioners knew most of the property owners and were very selective in the jurors that they chose. This process was later modified to include voting lists to create a more representative list of jurors. The jury pool is now selected at random from the voting lists by a jury administrator appointed by the judge. No longer are prospective jurors selected by jury commissioners who knew them and their qualifications to be jurors.

CHAPTER ELEVEN

Jury Selection
Steuben Circuit Court
July 1, 1975

The right to trial by jury developed as part of the English common law. The first English jurors were selected if possible from among persons who had witnessed the crime. How better to arrive at a fair and just verdict! Jurors usually did not take very long to arrive at a verdict. To insure promptness, no food or beverages were served to the jurors.

Traditionally jurors were "white property owning men." Qualification to be a juror was often tied to the right to vote. The original federal Constitution did not specify who was eligible to vote-this was left to the states to decide.

In the debates by the delegates to the 1850 Indiana Constitutional Convention a resolution was offered to grant "universal suffrage." One delegate stated, "According to our general understanding of the right of universal suffrage, I have no objection to the proposed resolution but if it be the intention of the mover of the resolution to extend the right of suffrage to females and Negroes, I am against it. 'All free white males over the age of twenty-one years'-I understand this language to be the measure of universal suffrage."

What "universal suffrage" meant in Indiana in 1851 was clearly set forth in the 1851 Indiana Constitution. Article 2, Section 2 states "Every white male citizen of the United States of age of twenty-one years and upwards—shall be entitled to vote." Section 5 states "No Negro or Mulatto shall have the right to suffrage."

The XV Amendment of the United States Constitution had granted the right to vote to male Negroes in 1870. In a delayed response thereto, in 1881 Article 2 of the Indiana Constitution was amended to delete the requirement of "white" and Article 5 was repealed. Male Negroes were thus granted the right to vote by Indiana law. The 1880 Indiana census listed "White, 1,938,798; Colored, 39,503, including 29 Chinese and 246 Indians and Half-Breeds."

Even though granted the right to vote, jury commissioners in examining the list of property owners and their perceived qualifications to serve as jurors would not select Negroes to serve as jurors for many years.

Women were granted the right to vote by the XIX Amendment of the United States Constitution in 1920 and by the Indiana Constitution in 1921. Even after the passage of these amendments women were still often excluded from jury service on the grounds that their primary duty was to take care of their homes and families. Even if women could vote, strong male prejudice (male jury commissioners) continued to dictate that they should not be chosen as the "raw material women might hear in the course of a criminal trial would shock their delicate sensibilities."

It was not until 1936, fifteen years after the Indiana Constitution specifically allowed women to vote, that the first women jurors served in Steuben County.

Although the common law of England was initially incorporated by Indiana courts, several basic changes were made including the qualifications of jurors. Jurisprudence in the United States has adopted the rigorous rule that jurors must not have any prior knowledge of the facts and must not have formed any opinions in regard to the facts or the guilt or innocence of the defendant.

In order to obtain such jurors, prospective jurors are questioned as to their qualifications before being selected to serve as a juror. The process of examination is called voir dire, a French phrase meaning "to speak the truth."

On July 1, 1975, at 9 a.m., with the defendant, all attorneys and forty prospective jurors present, the bailiff intoned, "All rise, the Honorable John R. Berger, presiding" and I entered the courtroom from a door behind my bench.

Traditionally the judge's bench and chair were raised about two steps. About twenty feet in front of the judge's bench were two large desks facing me. One was on the left for defense counsel, his assistant and the defendant, and one was on the right for the prosecutor, his assistant and the chief investigating officer. The twelve seat jury box was to the right at a right angle to the judge's bench. The witness box was just to the right of the bench. All testimony and proceedings would be taped or written in shorthand by the court reporter who sat just to the left of the bench in her own box.

Historically under the common law, a jury consisted of twelve members. The Constitution provides in the VI Amendment that all persons charged with a crime shall be granted an impartial jury trial. The Constitution does not specify how many members there must be on an impartial jury. The United States Supreme court decided in 1970 that a six member criminal jury for non capital crimes pursuant to a Florida statute was constitutional. Since then many states have passed legislation permitting less than a twelve member jury for certain crimes. Indiana in 1981 passed legislation requiring a twelve member jury for serious felonies and a six member jury for lesser felonies (Class D) and misdemeanors. A misdemeanor is usually classified as a crime providing for a sentence of one year imprisonment or less.

The voir dire examination in the Roberts case then began before a crowded and hushed courtroom.

With considerable apprehension and a quiet prayer, I was about to embark upon my greatest test as a judge.

I welcomed the prospective jurors. I then introduced myself, all attorneys, the defendant and the chief investigating officer. I explained briefly the charges, the possible penalties and the procedure that would follow.

First a jury of twelve with one alternate would be selected by voir dire examination. Those not chosen to be jurors would be excused. Then preliminary instructions will be given by me to the jury as to the charges against the defendant and the law which the jury should apply. The jury will then hear opening statements by the prosecutor and defense counsel. The presentation of evidence will then be made, first by the prosecutor and then by the defense. At the close of the evidence, the prosecutor and defense counsel will make closing arguments and I will give the jury final instructions. The jury will then retire to deliberate. During the trial, except for the time the jurors are in court, the jurors will be allowed to separate and carry out their normal lives.

Twelve of the prospective jurors were first seated in the twelve seat jury box and questioned. In some courts, the judge asks all of the questions. I took the traditional approach and allowed the attorneys to ask the questions. The questions were addressed to the initial twelve but all other prospective jurors were instructed by me to listen to the questions. If a juror was excused, another prospective juror was called forth and took the vacant seat in the jury box to be questioned.

Many courts now submit to prospective jurors several weeks prior to trial a jury questionnaire which must be answered under oath. These questionnaires contain basic questions concerning biographical background, prior experience with the law, law enforcement or the court system, ability to serve as a juror, and knowledge of the case and of any prospective witnesses. Some questionnaires are over fifty pages long and subject to presentation and argument before the judge prior to being agreed upon and submitted to the prospective jurors. The attorneys have the opportunity to examine the answers prior to trial to assist them in determining whether to accept or challenge a juror. The use of the questionnaire does not replace voir dire examination by the attorneys at trial but rather supplements and shortens the voir dire.

The 1994 O.J. Simpson questionnaire was seventy-five pages long and contained three hundred and two questions. It included the following questions.

"Please state your personal belief regarding each statement. Answer the following four questions by stating: Strongly agree? Agree? Strongly disagree? Disagree? No opinion?

1. If the prosecution goes to the trouble of bringing someone to trial, the person is probably guilty.

2. The testimony of law enforcement officers is not entitled to any greater or lesser weight merely because they are law enforcement officers.

3. Regardless of what the law says, a defendant in a criminal trial should be required to prove his or her innocence.

4. A defendant in a criminal trial should testify or produce some evidence to prove that he or she is not guilty.

5. How big a problem do you think racial discrimination against African-Americans is in Southern California. Serious? Somewhat serious? Not too serious? Not at all?

6. Have you ever experienced fear of an African-American? Explain.

7. How would you feel if a close family member married an African-American? Favor? Would not approve? Would oppose it? Explain.

8. What is your view concerning the reliability of the DNA analysis to accurately identify a person as the source of blood or hair found at a crime scene? Very reliable? Not very reliable? Somewhat reliable? Unreliable? Don't know?"

It would be interesting to know how the trial jurors under oath answered this last question as they found him not guilty in spite of the DNA evidence of his blood found at the scene which excluded only one out of one hundred and seventy million as a match.

The procedure for voir dire was to allow alternately the prosecuting attorney and defense counsel to question jurors as to their backgrounds and qualifications. By statute, jurors must be a voter, freeholder, householder, or spouse of a householder. Also, ferryman, policeman, fireman, veterinarians and dentists and those over 65 could be excused from jury service upon request. Grand jury qualifications were more restrictive by Indiana statute. A grand juror could not be insane or in the habit of becoming intoxicated but a regular (petit) juror could!

The voir dire examination of jurors by the attorneys provides an excellent opportunity for the attorneys by their questions to stress certain aspects of their case.

Roberts' attorney explained to each juror the doctrine of defendant's presumption of innocence that followed throughout the trial, and the rule that before conviction a juror must be convinced beyond a reasonable doubt that the defendant is guilty of the crime charged. Each juror was asked if he or she understood the doctrines and if he or she would be willing to accept and apply it. He asked this of all jurors and therefore it was emphasized over and over again.

Unlimited challenges to a juror by counsel "for cause" are permitted, examples of which are: the juror is related to a victim or a prospective witness or had an opinion as to guilt.

Also, in a murder case, each party had 20 "peremptory challenges" without cause. No explanation need be given to have a juror excused if peremptorily challenged. Peremptory challenges are made by counsel to try and shape the jury to favor their client. In some well

55

funded high profile cases, jury consultants are hired to advise counsel as to which jurors to accept or excuse.

In the Roberts case, defense counsel tried to eliminate women, educated, older, middle and upper class jurors. The prosecutor tried to retain such jurors. If this case had been tried in a metropolitan area with a large black population, perhaps peremptory challenges might have been used by the prosecutor to challenge black jurors. A later United States Supreme Court case declared unconstitutional the use of peremptory challenges for the sole purpose of excluding blacks.

The prospective imposition of the death sentence raised close questions concerning what views a juror could hold concerning such a sentence and not be subject to a challenge for cause.

If a juror stated that he or she could never vote for a death sentence, he or she would be excused for cause.

If however, a juror was generally opposed to the death sentence, this would not of itself be justification for a challenge for cause. A juror would be qualified if such a juror stated that he or she could possibly vote for the death sentence under a certain set of circumstances even though generally opposed. In the Roberts case there were several prospective jurors who were of this opinion and were not excused by me for cause. Even though not excused for cause, the prosecutor peremptorily challenged them.

In a death sentence case, the typical jury questionnaire asks questions concerning the above beliefs and often asks:

"Are you in favor of the death penalty as a punishment for crime? Explain.

Do you believe that the death penalty serves any legitimate purpose in our society? Yes? No? If so, what purpose: Punishment? Retribution? Deterrence? Prevention?"

The possibility of a death sentence also posed another problem in selecting a juror. Steuben County residents had rarely been exposed to a person accused of murder. They had never been asked to decide whether a person should be put to death. Several prospective jurors stated that they were not opposed to the death penalty but they could not make a decision that could lead to a death sentence. I excused such jurors for cause.

After a long day of voir dire examination, twelve prospective jurors were accepted by the defense. The cause was continued for further voir dire until the next morning. All prospective jurors were admonished by me to not discuss the case with any one and not to read any articles or listen to any radio or television reports. The jurors were then allowed to separate and directed to return to court at 9 a.m. the next morning, July 2.

During the entire voir dire examination, no questions were asked of the jurors by defense counsel as to a juror's opinion of African-Americans and if the juror could render a fair verdict when an African-American was the defendant and a white woman was the victim. Only the general question, "Is there any reason why you as a juror could not render a fair and impartial verdict" was asked.

CHAPTER TWELVE

Jury Selection
Steuben Circuit Court
July 2 and November 5, 1975

On the next day, July 2, 1975, before the jury assembled, defense counsel called to my attention an article published the previous day in the *Fort Wayne Journal Gazette*, a newspaper widely circulated and read in Steuben County.

The article described the trial about to begin in Angola and set forth in detail certain previous unrelated charges against Roberts. Such information would not be admissible at the trial and if read by any juror would be highly prejudicial to the defendant. Defense counsel then made a motion that the entire jury panel be dismissed. I questioned the prospective jurors as to whether any of them had read any article about the trial, and received answers from two jurors that they had read the article in the *Journal Gazette*. Since I had admonished the jurors not to read any articles, I was not certain that the responses of the other jurors that they had not read any articles were accurate. It would have been difficult for a juror to admit that the judge's admonishment was ignored. Because of this uncertainty and to eliminate any possibility of a tainted juror, I dismissed the entire panel. The cause was reset for trial on November 5, 1975.

On November 5, 1975, again with an overflow courtroom, forty prospective new jurors assembled and voir dire examination began. After two days of voir dire, twelve jurors with one alternate were accepted by both the prosecution and the defense. The jury then took an oath to "well and truly try and determine this cause at issue and now on trial and return a true verdict according to the law and the evidence as it is presented to you during this trial, so help you God."

The jury consisted of three women and nine men. The alternate was a woman. Each party seemed satisfied that it would be a fair and impartial jury (and maybe by their skillful use of peremptory challenges decide in their favor). After selection of the thirteen jurors and jurors

58

being peremptorily or for cause challenged and excused, only six remained of the original forty prospective jurors. The selected jurors were admonished, excused for the day and ordered to return at 9 a.m. on November 10.

If more jurors had been needed, the law provided that a judge could order the sheriff to go to any public place (the street in front of the courthouse) and select more prospective jurors from among the previously happy shoppers. They would have to immediately appear before the judge for jury service. This law has now been changed and no longer can the judge order bystanders to be jurors.

CHAPTER THIRTEEN

The Trial–Preliminary Instructions
Steuben Circuit Court
November 10, 1975

On November 10, 1975, the courtroom was again filled to capacity with others standing outside the large courtroom doors waiting for a vacant spectator seat. Security was high at all times when Roberts was present including four deputy sheriffs.

Roberts' two brothers and several friends were present throughout the trial. They were thoroughly searched by the deputy sheriffs before being allowed to enter the courtroom. One brother was overheard saying, "He won't be in jail much longer." No other Roberts' family members attended the trial.

William Harold's three brothers and Elizabeth Harold's sister attended the entire trial. However, since the Harold brothers would be witnesses, they could not be in the courtroom until after they had testified. The Harold's parents did not attend the trial. All members of the Harold family, except Elizabeth's sister, were also searched before entering the courtroom.

Charles Gantz and his supporting staff, prosecution witnesses, and involved police officers stayed during the entire trial at the new Holiday Inn five miles north of Angola near the Indiana Toll Road Angola exit. Tom Jones and David James Roberts stayed at the nearby Cedar Lodge, a small modest family owned (American) motel. The defense budget was limited by Judge Young and the Johnson County Commissioners who had to approve all defense expenditures.

Iona Crain, the court reporter, who lived in a house in the woods near the courthouse, remembers being so frightened during the trial that she kept all her blinds closed at night at her house.

I welcomed the jurors and commenced by reading to the jurors the Preliminary Instructions which included the murder and arson charges, and the fact that as to certain murder charges a second phase of the trial may be held to determine if the death sentence should be imposed.

60

I explained that the trial would be bifurcated to accomplish this. That meant that there would be two phases in the trial. The first would be the presentation of evidence as to the guilt or innocence of the accused on all counts. The second, in the event of a finding of guilt by the jurors on counts II, IV or V, would also be heard later by the same jury in order to decide if the death penalty would be imposed. At the death penalty hearing, the jury could consider additional evidence and statements of counsel.

The bifurcation procedure was not set forth in Indiana law at the time of the Roberts trial. I adopted this procedure however to keep certain evidence that may have been very prejudicial to the defendant that was admissible in the second life or death determination phase separate from the guilt or innocence phase of the trial.

I also read preliminary instructions to the jurors concerning the Presumption of Innocence-Burden of Proof, Reasonable Doubt, and Credibility of Witnesses-Weighing Evidence as follows:

PRESUMPTION OF INNOCENCE – BURDEN OF PROOF

Under the law of this State you must presume that the defendant is innocent. You must continue to believe he is innocent throughout the trial, unless the State proves that the defendant is guilty, beyond a reasonable doubt, of every essential element of the crimes charged.

Since the defendant is presumed to be innocent he is not required to present any evidence to prove his innocence, or to prove or explain anything. If, at the conclusion of the trial, there remains in your mind a reasonable doubt concerning the defendant's guilt, you must find him not guilty.

REASONABLE DOUBT

A "reasonable doubt" is a fair, actual and logical doubt that arises in your mind after an impartial consideration of all of the evidence and circumstances in this case. It should be a doubt based upon reason and common sense and not a doubt based upon imagination or speculation.

If, after considering all of the evidence, you have reached such a firm belief in the guilt of the defendant that you would feel safe to act upon that conviction, without hesitation, in a matter of the highest concern and importance to you, when you are not required to act at all, then you will have reached that degree of certainty which excludes reasonable doubt and authorizes conviction.

The rule of law which requires proof beyond a reasonable doubt applies to each juror individually. Each of you must refuse to vote for conviction unless you are convinced beyond a reasonable doubt of the defendant's guilt. Your verdict must be unanimous.

CREDIBILITY OF WITNESSES-WEIGHING EVIDENCE

You are the exclusive judges of the evidence, the credibility of any witness and the weight to be given to the testimony of each witness. In considering the testimony of any witness, you may take into account his or her ability and opportunity to observe; the memory, manner and conduct of the witness while testifying; any interest, bias or prejudice the witness may have; any relationship with other witnesses or interested parties; and the reasonableness of the testimony of the witness considered in the light of all of the evidence in this case.

You should attempt to fit the evidence to the presumption that the defendant is innocent and the theory that every witness is telling the truth. You should not disregard the testimony of any witness without a reason and without careful consideration. However, if you find that the testimony of a witness is so unreasonable as to be unworthy of belief, or if you find so much conflict between the testimony of witnesses that you cannot believe all of them, then you must determine which of the witnesses you will believe and which of them you will disbelieve.

In weighing the testimony to determine what or whom you will believe, you should use your own knowledge, experience and common sense gained from day to day living. You may find that the number of witnesses who testify to a particular fact, or one side or the other, or the quantity of evidence on a particular point does not control your determination of the truth. You should give the greatest weight to that evidence which convinces you most strongly of its truthfulness.

CHAPTER FOURTEEN

The Trial-The State's Evidence Day 1
November 10, 1975

After I read the preliminary instructions to the jury, Charles Gantz and Tom Jones made opening statements to the jury.

Opening statements are used by attorneys to ingratiate themselves with the jurors and to set forth their case. The prosecutor goes first and then defense counsel.

Charles Gantz carefully described the crimes charged and the possible penalties including death. He outlined the witnesses that he would call and the testimony that he expected to elicit. He described the exhibits that he would offer into evidence and their relevancy. He stated that the jurors represented the conscience of the community and, even though it would be a most difficult task for them, he was convinced that, after hearing all of the evidence, the jury would do their duty and find David James Roberts guilty of all charges.

Tom Jones gave a brief statement reminding the jury that, as the judge had instructed, they must presume that the defendant did not commit any crime and that they should not form any opinions as to guilt or innocence until they had heard all of the evidence. He stated that the defendant did not have to prove his innocence and that the entire burden was upon the prosecution to prove the guilt of defendant beyond a reasonable doubt. He stated that, after they had heard all of the evidence, he believed strongly that they would not find Roberts guilty of any charged crime.

In a criminal trial, the prosecutor presents the state's evidence, subject to cross examination, first. Next the defense counsel presents evidence subject to cross examination. The prosecutor then may present evidence in rebuttal.

Upon motion of counsel, all prospective witnesses, except the chief investigating officer, Lt. Robert Allen, were separated from the courtroom and admonished by me to not discuss their testimony with anyone until after the trial. The purpose of separation of witnesses is to prevent a prospective witness from hearing any prior or future proposed testimony and possibly altering their testimony to comply with the other testimony.

The jurors had been instructed by me as to the law and had heard the opening statements of the prosecution and defense. It was now time for them to hear the evidence.

In the first phase of the trial the prosecution had to present evidence to convince the jury beyond a reasonable doubt that the defendant had:

Intentionally killed William and Elizabeth Ann Harold with malice (ill will) and premeditation (intended to kill in advance of the killing) which required a life sentence and/or

Killed William and Elizabeth Ann Harold while committing Burglary (breaking and entering a dwelling with intent to commit Murder or Arson) which required a life sentence and under certain circumstances (to be determined in phase two of the trial) a death sentence and/or

Caused the death of Jenny Harold as a result of Arson (intentionally and maliciously burning any part of a house) which required a life sentence and under certain circumstances (to be determined in phase two of the trial) a death sentence and/or

Committed Arson.

When any witness was called to testify, I would have the witness stand before me and the bench, and raise his or her right hand. I would also raise my right hand, look directly into the eyes of the witness and say, "Do you swear or affirm that the testimony that you are about to give in this matter is the truth, the whole truth and nothing but the truth, so help you God or you do so affirm?" Upon an "I do" from the witness I would ask the witness to be seated in the witness box (the stand).

During the first phase of the trial the prosecutor presented forty-five witnesses.

The actual testimony of each witness or a summary thereof is presented below.

Prior to trial I had no knowledge of the facts in this case. I knew the charges that had been filed and the fact that there had been a bail hearing at which the prosecutor had failed to present sufficient evidence to have Roberts held without bail. Other than that, I was just like a thirteenth juror about to hear the evidence.

The State's first witness was **Gary Harter**.

DIRECT EXAMINATION BY MR. GANTZ:

Q. Please state your name.

A. Gary Harter.

Q. How old are you?

A. Twenty-six.

Q. Where did you live on January 19th, 1974?

A. In New Whiteland, Indiana.

Q. Calling your attention to the evening of January 19th, 1974, did you have occasion to be in the vicinity of Pine Drive in New Whiteland.

A. Yes.

Q. Please describe what you did and saw that night and early the next morning.

A. Well, I had been out with my girlfriend, who is now my wife, and we had been to a show. I took her home, which was at 719 Pine Drive, and we watched TV for a while. I left and came back to her house at about 1 a.m. and we watched TV some more. I left at about 4:30 in the morning to go home. When I was driving by the Harold house I noticed smoke coming from the house. I contacted a friend of mine, Deputy Adams, who was cruising in the neighborhood. I told him there was a house on fire on Pine and he said "Okay" and went on. He must have notified the fire department 'cause they showed up a few minutes later.

Q. Then what did you do or see?

A. We both ended up at the Harold house. We went up and looked around the house, and beat on the windows, to see if anybody was in there, and couldn't find anybody. We couldn't hear nobody or see anything through the windows.

Q. Well, now at the time you left your girlfriend's house, who is now your wife, could that have been earlier than 4:30?

MR. JONES: I am going to object to that, Your Honor. This is his witness. He can't impeach him as to his testimony.

THE COURT: It's overruled. You may answer.

A. Not much before that.

Q. Did you see flames when you first saw the house?

A. Yeah, very small flames coming out the side window.

That's all I have from this witness.

MR. JONES: I have no questions.

MR. GANTZ: At this time Your Honor, we would call **Charles Long** to the stand.

DIRECT EXAMINATION BY MR. GANTZ:

Q. Please state your name and address.

A. My name is Charles Long and I live in New Whiteland.

Q. What is your occupation, sir?

A. Assistant Fire Chief of the New Whiteland Volunteer Fire Department.

Q. And what are your duties?

A. I direct men at the fire and investigate fires.

Q. Did you have reason to investigate a fire on the 20th day of January, 1974, at 915 Pine Street in New Whiteland, Indiana, belonging to William and Elizabeth Ann Harold?

A. Yes.

Q. Can you relate to the court and to the jury what you did?

A. When we first got to the scene the fire was going and we-I later went to the hospital with the baby that we removed from the house.

Q. When did you arrive at the scene, sir?

A. Approximately 4:38 on the morning of the 20th.

Q. Okay, and what did you do upon arrival?

A. I was directing the fire trucks and laying out and connecting the hoses.

Q. What observations did you make?

A. There were flames showing from the front window of the house.

Q. Where were the flames?

A. They were coming from the top of the window of the middle room which was used as a den or television room.

Q. What did you do next?

A. When the fire equipment arrived I was at the ambulance and when they brought the baby up from behind the house we put the baby in the ambulance and I went with the baby in the ambulance to the Johnson County Hospital.

Q. Do you know if the baby was alive or dead when you were in the ambulance?

MR JONES: Now show our objection to that, Your Honor, unless there is some foundation for such an opinion. I think the cause of death requires an expert opinion.

MR. GANTZ: I did not ask for the cause of death. I asked if the baby was dead.

THE COURT: I think you could ask the witness if she had any symptoms of life or death.

Q. Well, were there any such symptoms?

A. I could not say because I was not in the back of the ambulance with the baby.

Q. Was the baby crying or moving?

A. No.

Q. What did you do next?

A. I returned to the scene of the fire at about 5:00 o'clock and entered the room where the two bodies were. It was the den.

Q. What did you see then?

A. The body of a male victim laying face down on the floor, feet next to the door, his head toward the television set in the corner. There was a gas can sitting right next to his shoulder. The body of the female person laying crossways of the room with her feet on the couch face down.

Q. Were the bodies clothed or not clothed?

A. The female body appeared not to be clothed. The male body looked like it had clothes on the underneath side and they had been burnt off the top-or the back side, I mean. There was burned clothing piled on top of each body.

Q. Did you observe anything else in the room?

A. Yes. There had been a fire burning in various places in the room and around the door and out into the hallway. The chair and couch was also burned pretty badly.

Q. Did you observe other fire damage in the house?

A. Yes. There was fire damage to the wall outside the den, to the hallway leading to the kitchen, and toward the living room. There was fire damage to the rug running out to the living room and in the living room. There was a lot of heat damage and the drapes in the front room had caught fire and burned. There was smoke and heat damage which caused peeling of wallpaper and this sort of thing in other rooms in the house.

Q. Did you observe any clocks?

A. There was a clock in the hallway that leads to the kitchen. The cord on that clock had burned in two. The clock was stopped at approximately four o'clock.

MR GANTZ: No further questions.

CROSS EXAMINATION BY MR JONES:

Q. Mr. Long did you observe a bathroom in the residence?

A. Yes.

Q. Isn't it a fact, Mr. Long, that in that bathroom there was a bath tub filled to bath level with water?

A. There was water in the tub, I'm not sure of the exact depth of it, sir.

Q. And the female body was nude?

A. Yes, sir, as far as I know.

MR. JONES: No further questions.

MR. GANTZ: No redirect examination.

The State will call **John Lasiter**.

DIRECT EXAMINATION BY MR. GANTZ:

Q. Please state your name, residence and occupation.

A. I am John Lasiter. I live in Johnson County and am a Deputy Sheriff of Johnson County. My rank is Detective Lieutenant.

Q. Did you have occasion to investigate a fire on the morning of January 20, 1974, at the Harold residence on 915 Pine Drive in New Whiteland, Indiana?

A. Yes, sir.

Q. What time did you arrive at the scene and what did you do?

A. I arrived at approximately 5:05 a.m. Shortly after I arrived the draperies in the living room re-ignited and was extinguished by the fire department. I entered the house and went to the family room or den where I visually viewed two bodies. The male body was lying parallel to the south wall of the room. The female body was lying parallel and at right angle to the west wall with one leg on the couch. There was burned clothing over the top of the female body. The female was naked. There was debris from the room over most of the male body.

Q. Did you know the subjects that were dead in that house?

A. I knew them by name at that time-knew who lived there.

Q. What further observations did you make concerning the den or TV room?

A. The TV room was charred from obvious fire damage and had a strong odor of gasoline. I observed a five gallon metal can. There was no male clothing in any of the closets in the TV room. There were several neckties knotted together on the chair and floor. There was a chair with several partially burned personal items on the seat-papers such as payment books, checkbook, and the victim's wallet or purse. All of these items were turned over to Officer Flint for safe keeping.

Q. Was there any money or currency in the wallet or purse.

A. No.

Q. What other observations did you make concerning other rooms in the house?

A. There was a small room in the back that had a cot and several barbells, weight lifting devices. There was a partially filled beer bottle on a small table. The room was heavily damaged by the fire. In the master bedroom there was a rack with several guns and a bow and arrow set. In the infant's room there was a crib. In the bathroom the tub was filled to bath level and the water had a heavy smoke skim across the top. Between the living room and the kitchen was a plastic and wood room divider which had not been burned and was lying on the floor.

Q. Did you observe anything with regards to the front living room?

A. Yes. There was a ladies coat and a diaper bag in a chair near the front door. There was some fire and smoke damage. There was an area of heavy fire damage on the rug, kind of like a fire trail, leading from near the front door to the TV room where the Harold bodies were. At the start of the trail in the living room near the front door there was a metal cap which we later found fit the gas can we found in the TV room. It was a cap with a long flexible pouring spout. Next to the spout we found a book of matches and a pair of black leather men's work gloves.

MR. GANTZ: That's all I have for this witness.

CROSS EXAMINATION BY MR. JONES:

Q. Okay, now Lieutenant, did you search the house the day you were up there?

A. The best we could do under the conditions.

Q. Did you find any male clothing in the closet of the master bedroom?

A. Yes. There was several shirts, a uniform type pants of blue wash and iron material. There were no sports coats or suits.

Q. Were there any sport coats or suits in any closets in the entire house?

A. If my memory serves me correctly, no, there were none.

Q. Tell us whether or not you found any money in the entire residence.

A. We found no currency or coins in the house if my memory serves me correctly.

Q. Did you ever investigate a burglary case?

A. Yes, many.

Q. In the course of your career as a policeman in Johnson County, isn't it a fact that this had many of the earmarks of a first degree burglary case?

A. With the exception of no forced entry that we found.

Q. There was no forced entry at all, was there?

A. Not that we found, no sir.

Q. In other words, whoever went into that house that night forced open no windows or doors that you could find, isn't that correct?

A. That's correct.

Q. And when you got there, the front door was standing wide open?

A. That's true. The screen door was closed though.

Q. Now you indicated that there was a partition that had been knocked down before the fire?

A. Yes there was.

Q. So what you are telling us is that there was a struggle back over in this room, wasn't there?

A. That was my opinion.

Q. Well, we've got a struggle and a bathtub full of water and neckties knotted together and money missing, but no forcible entry, right?

A. I don't know that there was money missing because I don't know that there was money in there before.

Q. Your investigation showed that they had been out that evening-been to a movie, had some pizza, a couple of beers before they came home. This indicates that probably there was some money or change in the house when they got home.

A. All I know was that we did not find any money.

Q. Did you know William Harold prior to his death?

A. Yes.

Q. Did he work out with weights and was he a person who could probably take care of himself?

A. Yes, sir.

Q. Now, in the course of your investigation did you receive information that the house had been broken into prior to January 19th and that two men's suits had been taken?

A. Yes I did.

Q. My point being, Lieutenant, that there was a breakin that same house, wasn't there?

A. Yes, sir.

Q. Okay. Now, in the course of your investigation, did you determine whether or not there had been any black people rent a room at the Ruby's Motel four- tenths of a mile east from the Harold house in New Whiteland?

A. Yes sir, I did.

Q. Tell the Jury what your investigation disclosed as to when these negroes or blacks arrived at the motel.

A. I interviewed the owner and he stated that two black males and two black females rented separate rooms from January 20, 1974, at 12:30 a.m. and left at 3:30 a.m. I showed him a series of photos including one of Roberts and they were negative.

Q. Did he tell you any reason at all why these negroes or blacks would have left that motel at 3:30 in the morning?

A. No, sir, they did not.

Q. Incidentally that's half an hour before the clock stopped up there at Pine Drive, isn't it?

A. That's correct.

Q. Now in the course of your investigation did you determine that a black male, or negro male, was seen at the Harold residence driving a light tan or gold big type automobile about 6:30 a.m. the morning of the fire?

A. Yes.

Q. The exact same type of car that you eventually looked for in connection with David Roberts, isn't that correct?

A. That's correct.

71

Q. Did you determine the identity of the black man who drove that car?

A. The volunteer fireman who saw the black man was shown six photos including a photo of David Roberts. He said if he had to pick out one of the people, it would probably be the photo of a person named Douglas Milford, not David Roberts.

MR. JONES: I have nothing further.

RE-DIRCT BY MR. GANTZ:

Q. Isn't it a fact that you received many leads in this case.

A. Yes, sir.

Q. And isn't it a fact that these leads led nowhere?

A. That's correct.

Q. Did you find any leads which led elsewhere than to David James Roberts?

A. No, sir.

Q. Isn't it a fact that there were many valuables in the house including the guns and they were not taken or missing?

A. That's true.

Q. Did you attach any significance to the fact that there might have been a prior burglary and that a person named Douglas Milford may have driven by the Harold house the morning of the fire?

A. Yes. We investigated further. We could find no leads on the burglary and determined that, in my own mind, Douglas Milford was not involved in the murders.

Mr. GANTZ: No further questions

Some jurors wondered why the police had a photograph of David James Roberts. At this point in the evidence there had been no evidence connecting him to the murders.

RE-CROSS BY MR. JONES:

Q. All right. You don't think that this burglary was significant or that another person was identified at the Harold house that morning other than the defendant, or this business about the bathtub being full, none of that you felt was too significant?

A. It cleared up the fact that there were no suits at the Harold house.

Q. So you did not follow up on any of this?

A. I personally did not follow up on the burglary.

Q. You had your suspect, didn't you?

A. Well, I-

Q. You weren't looking for somebody other than Roberts, were you?

A. Yes, we were.

MR. JONES: Nothing further.

Mark Flint, Johnson County Deputy Sheriff was next called by Mr. Gantz.

He testified as to the following:

He arrived at the scene at 4:41 a.m. He observed smoke and fire coming from the Harold house. He went around the house looking in the windows and observed a baby crib in the back bedroom. With the assistance of a fireman, he broke through the window and retrieved the baby, Jenny Harold. He went with her in the ambulance to the Johnson County Memorial Hospital and on the way administered cardiovascular resuscitation, closed heart massage and mouth to mouth resuscitation. They arrived at the hospital in about four minutes. Emergency doctors worked with the child for about fifteen minutes and then declared her dead.

He returned to the scene and took photographs of the house showing the fire damage, a small tract house built on a slab. He also took photographs of every room in the house, the gun rack, the crib, the bodies, the fire damage, the knotted neckties, the gas can, the cap and nozzle, the matches, the black gloves, the checkbook, wallet and purse, and the turned over room divider. He also testified as to placing hair samples from William and Elizabeth Harold which he had received from the coroner in plastic bags. He also obtained a sample of the liquid which was in the gas can. There was between two and three gallons of gas left in the can. He testified that he turned all samples and the gas can over to the sheriff's property room. He stated that he had been in control of all photographs and that they accurately represented what he had seen. The photographs were entered into evidence and shown to the jury.

1. Photograph of William Harold body in den

2. Photograph of Elizabeth Harold body in den

3. Photograph of gun rack

4. Photograph of crib

5. Photograph of gas can nozzle

6. Photograph of gas can in den

The photographs are as follows:

PHOTOGRAPH OF WILLIAM HAROLD IN DEN

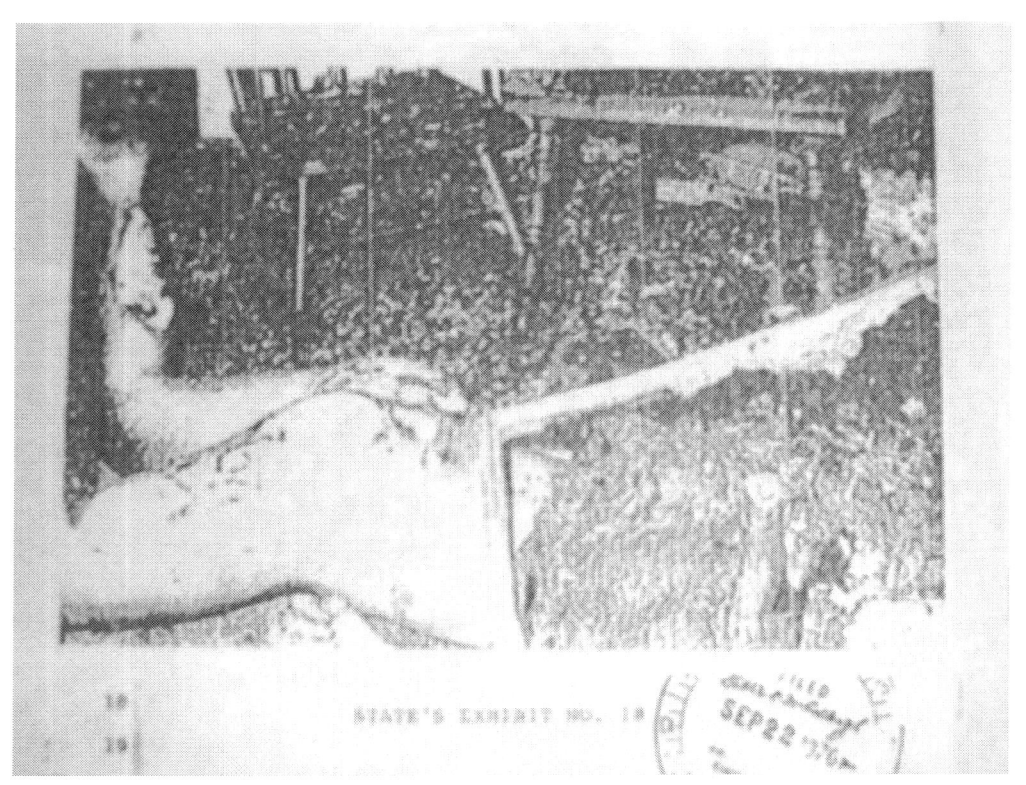

PHOTOGRAPH OF ELIZABETH HAROLD IN DEN

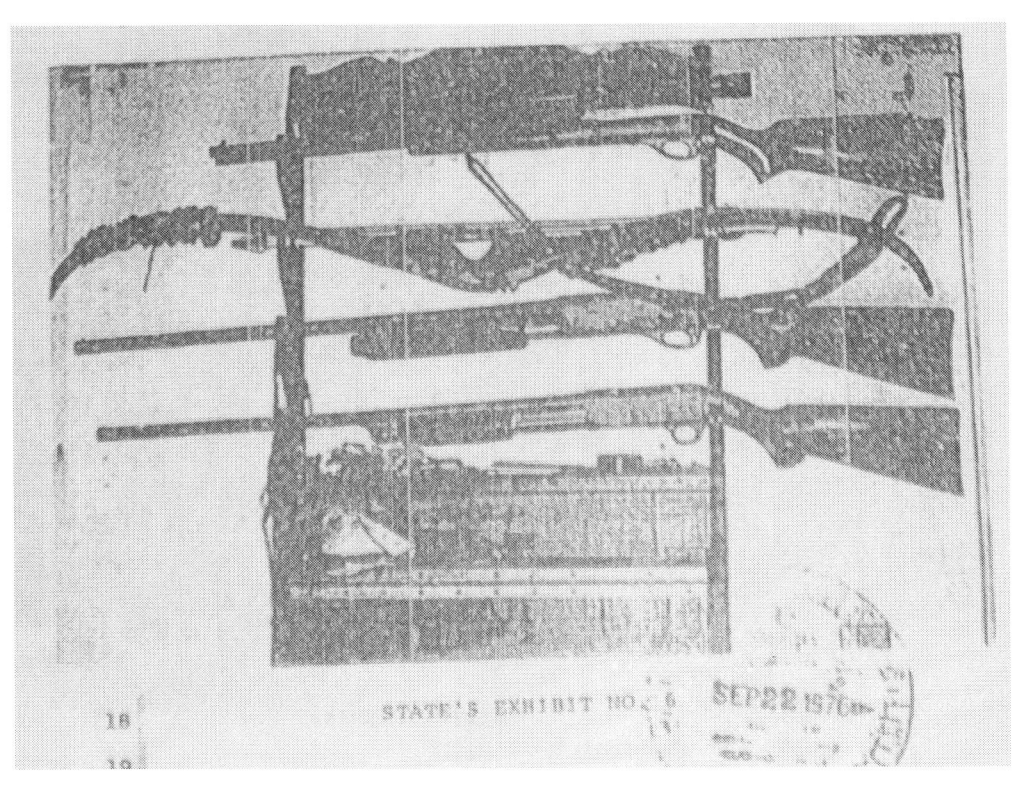

PHOTOGRAPH OF GUN RACK

PHOTOGRAPH OF JENNY'S CRIB

GAS CAN NOZZLE FOUND NEAR FRONT DOOR

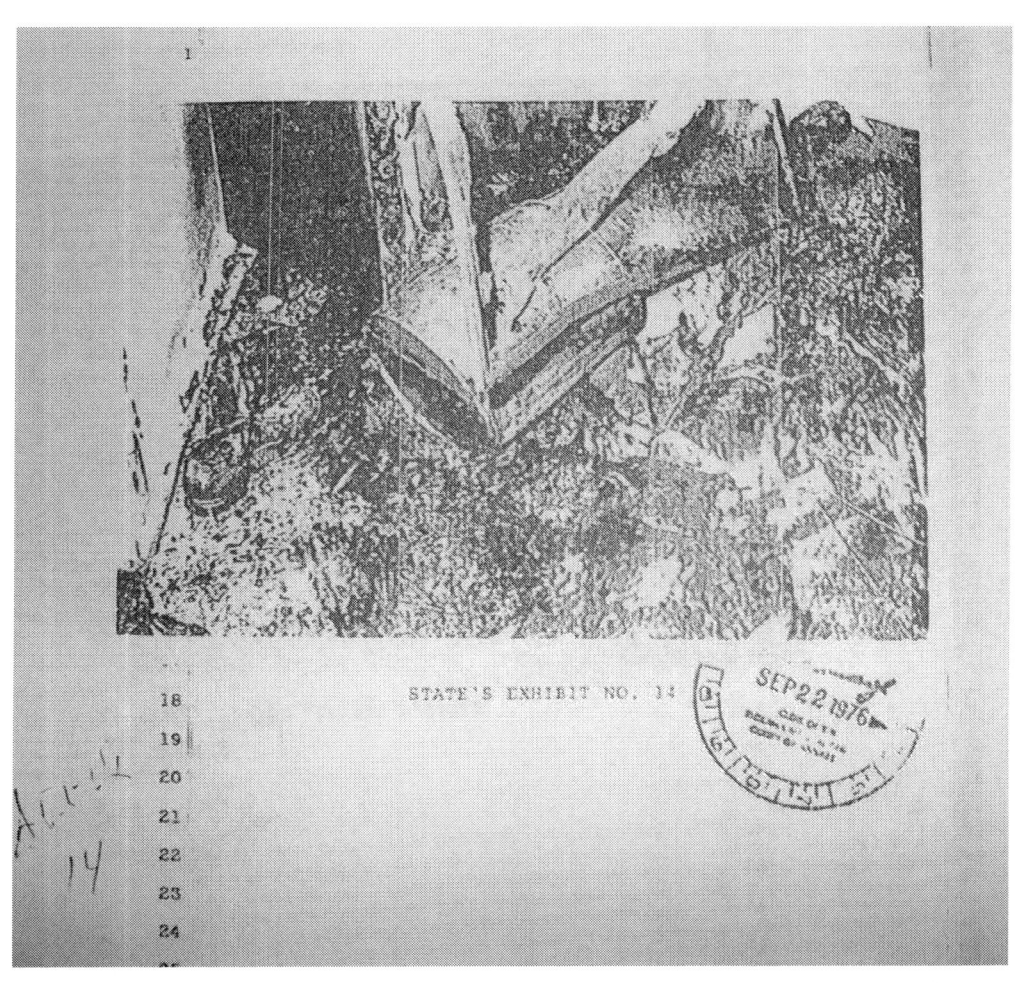

STATE'S EXHIBIT NO. 14   SEP 22 1976

RED GAS CAN FOUND IN DEN

He also testified that he had taken photographs during the autopsy. These photographs were to be offered into evidence when the doctor performing the autopsies testified.

He was asked upon cross examination if he had taken any footprint imprints, or if he had attempted to take any fingerprints within the house, on the gas can and nozzle, or front door knob. He stated that he had not.

Upon re-direct by Mr. Gantz, he stated that there were hundreds of footprints from the firemen and officers and therefore it was impossible to determine any individual footprints. Also the wet and sooty conditions did not allow valid fingerprints to be taken.

Deputy Sheriff **Joe Barger** then testified that he was in charge of the property room and that the exhibits and materials obtained by Mark Flint were turned in to him and that the same property was at all times in his possession until brought to the court.

All physical items observed at the scene including the red five gallon gas with "$5 Deposit" in yellow crayon, the gas can nozzle, purse, wallet, checkbook, ties, matches and gloves were identified and admitted into evidence.

There was no further testimony from these witnesses.

Winfrey Burton, Town Marshall of New Whiteland, was the next witness. He testified that he had been at the scene at about 5: 30 a.m. on the 20th of January and had observed the burned house and two bodies. He staked out the house with police ribbons. He also called the coroner, Dr. Palmer, to come to the scene. He then visited with a brother of the Harolds and determined that the older daughter, Marie, had been with the brother. He further testified to obtaining an arrest warrant for David James Roberts and arresting him on January 26, 1974. Marshall Burton also made arrangements for a 1970 gold and tan Buick Riviera found at Roberts' residence to be impounded. A search warrant was then obtained to search the vehicle and the registration of the vehicle in the name of David James Roberts was found in the glove compartment. The registration was admitted into evidence.

At the conclusion of this testimony I adjourned the court for the day. I allowed the jurors to separate (to go home and not be sequestered) and admonished them not to discuss the case with anyone, not to read, see or listen to any accounts of the trial, and not to form any opinion as to guilt or innocence until they had heard all of the evidence, the final statements of counsel, my final instructions as to the law applicable to this case, and had an opportunity to deliberate with fellow jurors.

I thanked the jurors and told them to return the next day at 8 a.m.

At this point in the trial the jurors have heard no evidence connecting Roberts to the burglary, arson and murders. The jurors were wondering why Roberts was arrested.

CHAPTER FIFTEEN
The Trial-The State's Evidence Day 2
November 11, 1975

At 8 a.m. the next morning, November 11, 1975, trial resumed. It was Veteran's Day but I decided not to take a break. Further evidence was presented by the prosecutor.

The first witnesses were **Dr. Harley Palmer**, Johnson County Coroner and **Dr. Russell Benz**, forensic pathologist from Marion County General Hospital who performed the autopsies on William, Elizabeth Ann and Jenny Harold on January 21, 1974. They described in detail the findings. Dr. Palmer's testimony as to cause of death was:

Q. Dr. what is your opinion as to the cause and manner of death of William Harold, Elizabeth Ann Harold and Jenny Harold?

A. Well, as to William and Elizabeth, they died of asphyxia.

Q. What exactly is asphyxia?

A. Asphyxia is the same as a smothering type of death-it's a lack of oxygen. It may be produced in several ways.

Q. And what are the ways in which asphyxia can be accomplished?

A. There are numerous ways to obstruct the nasal or nose passage and the mouth passages, any one of which would produce asphyxia.

Q. What about compression of the neck-would that be a way?

A. Yes, sir.

Q. Can you say what method of asphyxia was used on Elizabeth Harold?

A. Yes. She had bruising inside her neck structures. She had hemorrhages in her eyes-all very characteristic of a smothering type of suffocation. She was smothered or strangled.

Q. How about William Harold?

A. He had small hemorrhages within his eyes which is also consistent with asphyxia by smothering. He was smothered or strangled.

83

Q. Could knotted neckties or two inch wide tape have been used to strangle Elizabeth Harold or close her mouth?

A. That is possible.

Q. Okay. Now in your opinion were William and Elizabeth Harold's deaths caused by accidental means?

A. No, sir.

Q. And what was the cause of death of Jenny Harold?

A. She died of smoke inhalation and carbon monoxide intoxication.

Q. Was her death accidental?

A. No, sir.

Q. In your opinion Doctor, were William Harold and Elizabeth Harold dead when they were set on fire?

A. Yes.

Q. What else did you observe as to the condition of the bodies of William and Elizabeth Harold?

A. There were various bruises, abrasions or hemorrhages on the forehead, eye, nose, chin and necks on both of them.

Q. Are such conditions indicative of having been attacked or hit by someone-of a struggle or fight?

A. Yes, sir.

Q. Doctor, were you able to determine if Elizabeth Harold had been raped?

A. No, I was not. Because of her burned condition it was not possible to make any such determination.

CROSS EXAMINATION BY MR. JONES:

Q. Now Doctor, the tape, the knotted neckties, the asphyxia, the bruises and other conditions of the bodies in no way indicate to you who is the guilty party-you'll agree with that, won't you?

A. That's correct.

Q. You don't have any idea about that?

A. That's right, sir.

Q. All you know is that these people died-shall we say of unnatural causes?

A. Unnatural causes, yes, sir.

Dr. Benz testified that he had observed injuries on Elizabeth Harold's wrists which were consistent with her arms being bound. He also observed marks on the mouth of Elizabeth Harold possibly from having tape removed.

Many large color photographs of the autopsy showing multiple views of the bodies before the autopsy and during each stage of the autopsy were offered as evidence. Defense counsel objected to the introduction of the photographs claiming that defendant admits the death and cause of death of the victims and that the only purpose of introducing the photographs was to inflame the passions of the jury against the defendant. I carefully examined each photograph and admitted only six as follows:

1. Morgue view of Elizabeth Harold body (back side)
2. Morgue view of Elizabeth Harold body (face and neck)
3. Morgue view of William Harold body (back side)
4. Morgue view of William Harold body (face and neck)
5. Morgue view of Jenny Harold body
6. Blackened throat and lung of Jenny Harold at autopsy

Photographs 1, 3, and 5 are as follows:

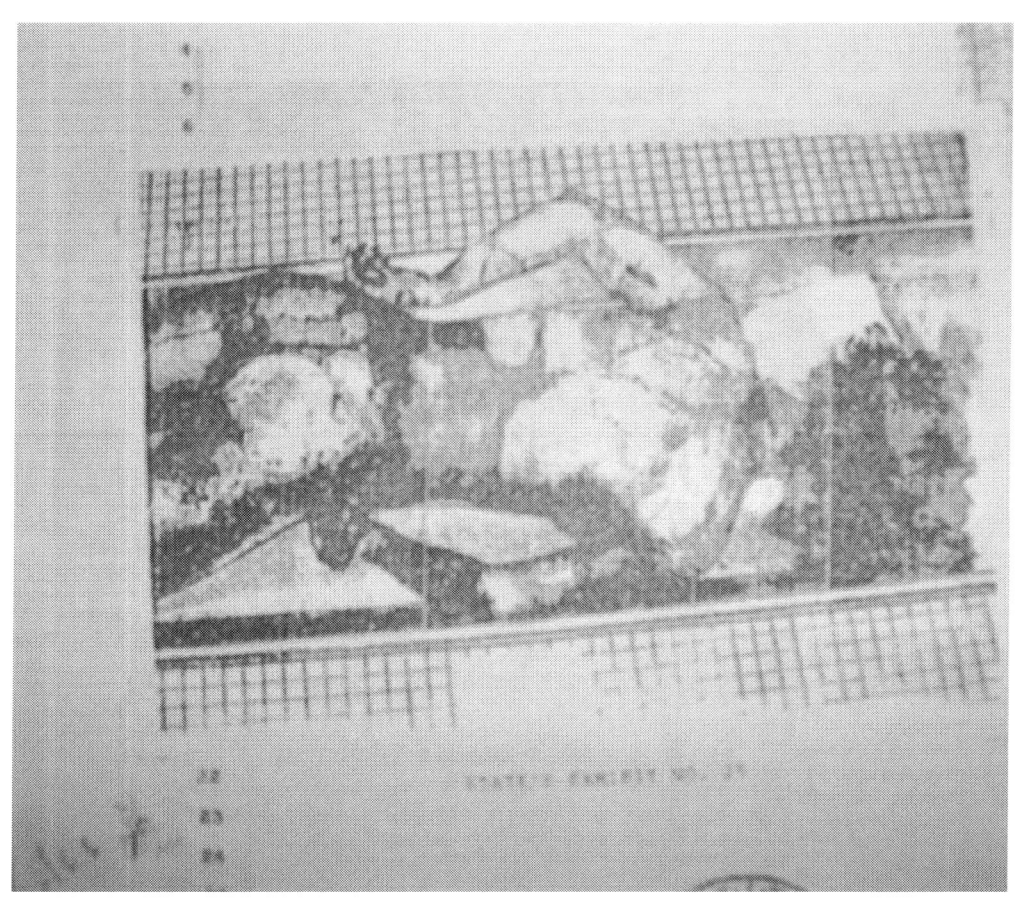

AUTOPSY PHOTOGRAPH OF ELIZABETH HAROLD

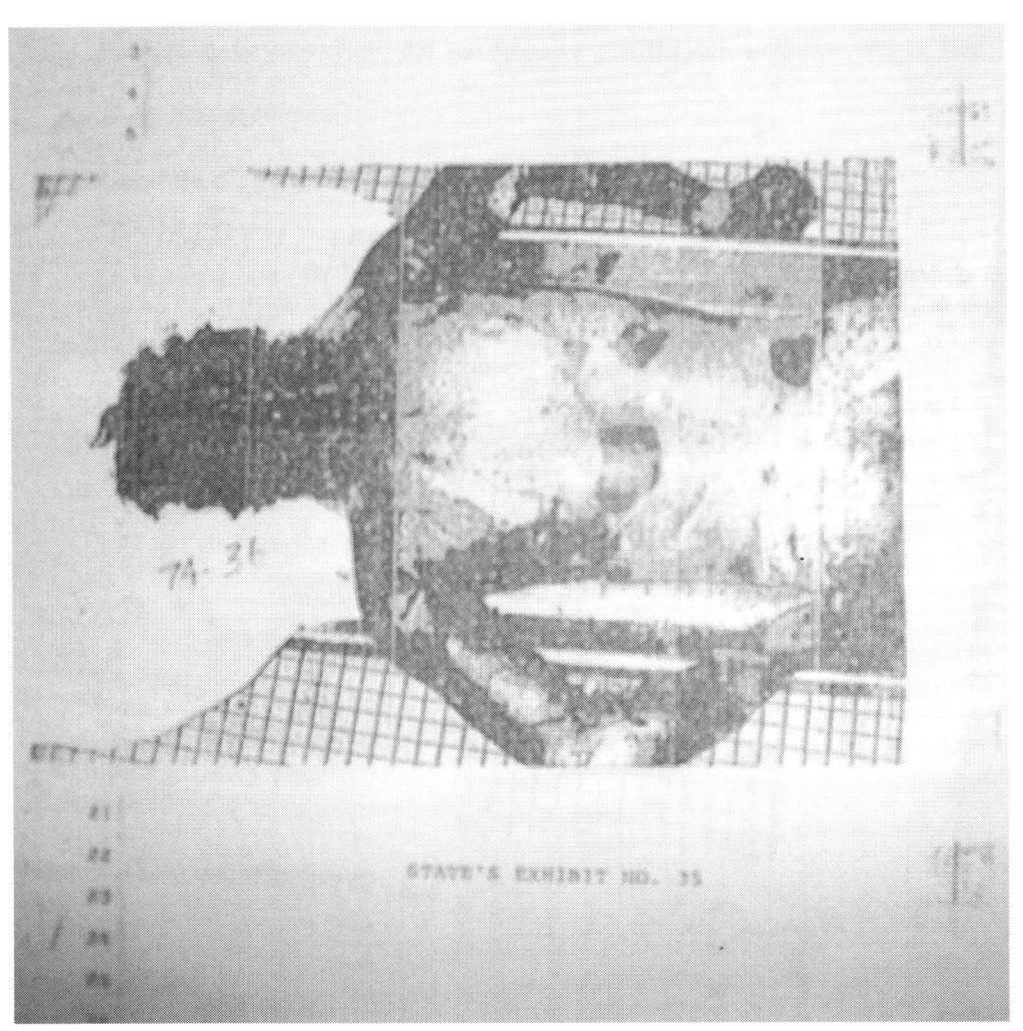

AUTOPSY PHOTOGRAPH OF WILLIAM HAROLD

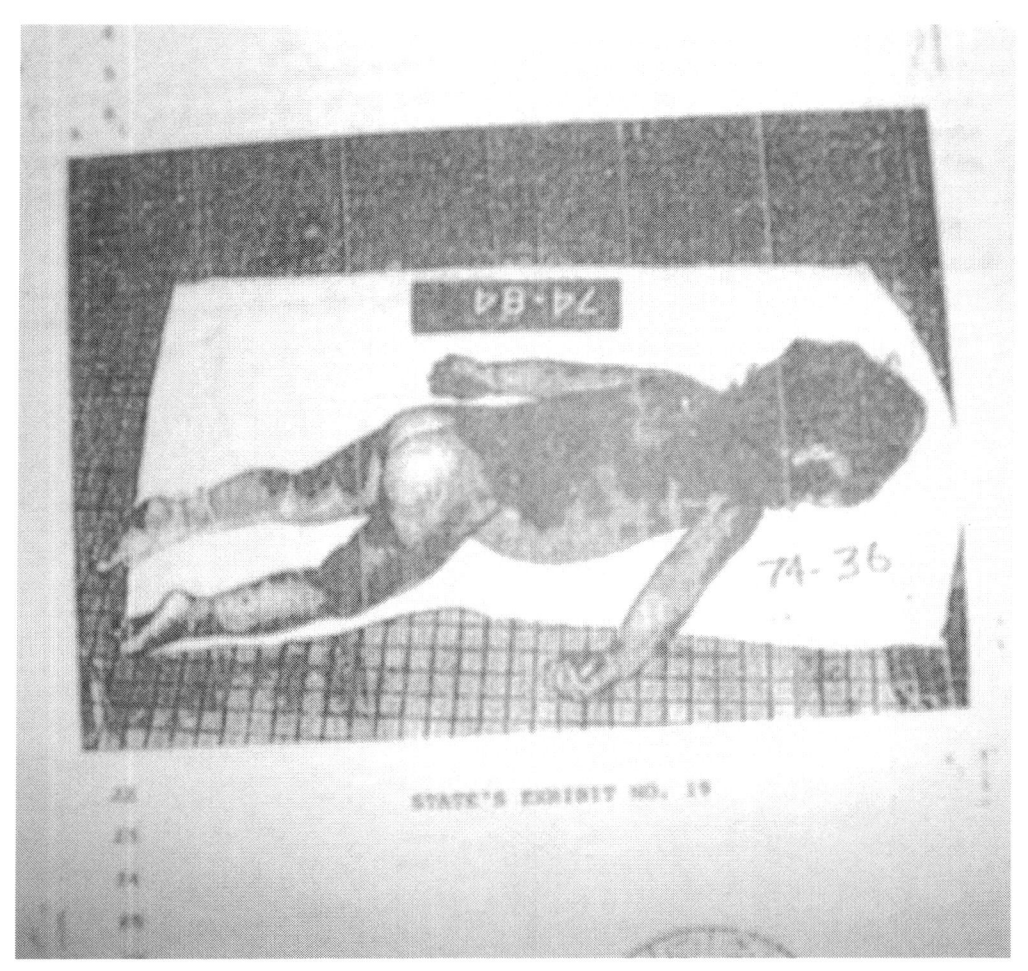

AUTOPSY PHOTOGRAPH OF JENNY HAROLD

The next witness was **Dee Corbin** of the Indiana State Police Fire Marshal's Office. He testified as to his extensive training and schooling in fire investigation and eighteen years of experience. He stated that he arrived at the scene at 7 a.m. the morning of the 20th and had made a complete examination of the Harold house. His opinion was that the fire was caused by gasoline igniting and that the inflammable had been contained in the red five gallon gas can found in the den. He stated that it definitely was arson. He testified as to a fire trail on the rug from the living room near the front door, where the gas can nozzle and match book were present, and leading down the hallway into the den or TV room. It was apparent to him that gasoline had also been poured on the Harolds' bodies and around the den. He estimated that the fire temperature was between 1600 and 1800 degrees.

He gave his opinion that the arsonist may have started pouring the gasoline on the rug in the living room, then down the hallway, and ended up in the den where he poured gasoline on the bodies and around the den. He left the gas can in the den assuming that it would be burned and unrecognizable and returned to the living room. He then set fire to the beginning of the gas trail and left through the front door.

He testified that he had watched Deputy Mark Flint make a drawing of the den which was an accurate representation. The drawing was admitted into evidence and is as follows:

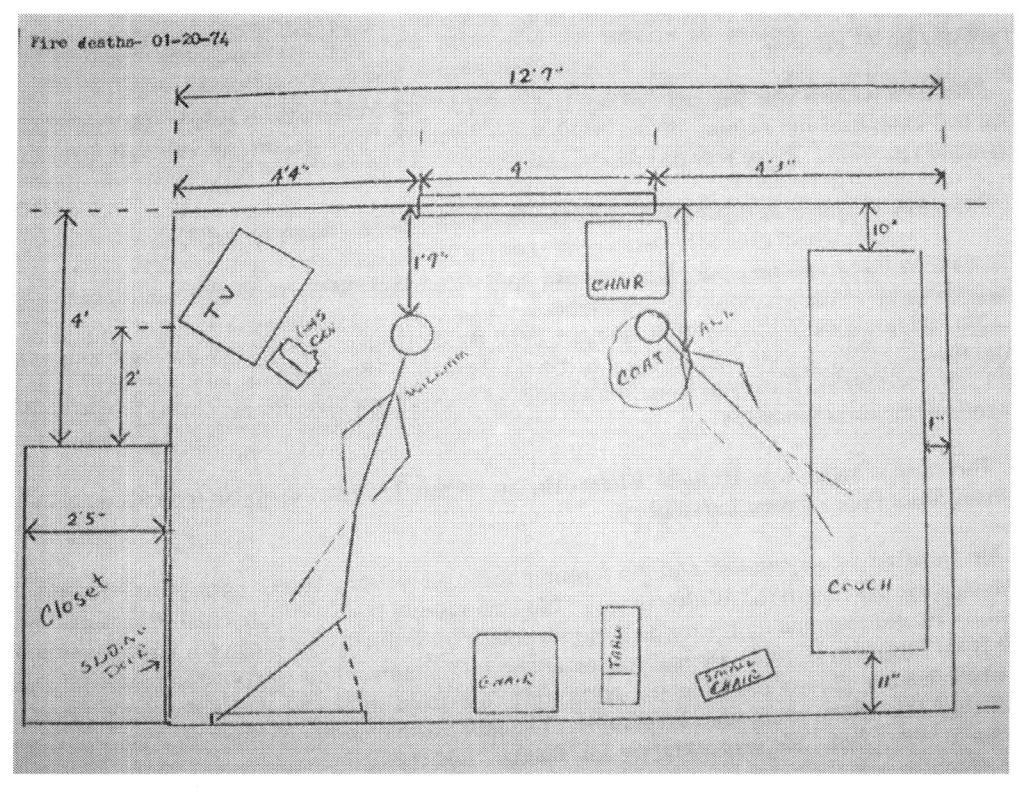

DIAGRAM OF DEN

There was a vigorous cross examination by defense counsel Albert Friend. The witness did not change his opinion.

The next witness was **Russell Forbes**, a chemist for the Indiana State Police. He testified that he had examined the sample of the fluid taken from the five gallon gas can and that it was premium gasoline. There was no cross examination.

Sherrill Anspagh of the Indiana State Police then testified.

He also had examined the Harold house and stated that effective fingerprints could not be taken because of the wet condition and soot.

He had searched Roberts' gold and tan 1970 Buick Riviera automobile pursuant to a search warrant. In addition to the registration to David James Roberts he found a hair fiber near the gas pedal and turned it over to Ronald Eltzeroth of the Indiana State Police Crime Laboratory for examination and comparison.

The next witness was **Ronald Eltzeroth**, an expert forensic scientist who worked in the Indiana State Police Crime Laboratory.

He testified to examining and performing tests on various items turned over to him by investigating officers in the Roberts case. No hair sample from Roberts had been turned over to him. He did examine hair samples from the heads of William and Elizabeth Harold and pubic hair from Elizabeth Harold. He had compared them to a human hair sample obtained from a pair of black leather gloves found at the scene near the front door and the hair sample found in Roberts' car. They were not comparable. The hair sample on the gloves ranged in color from brown to very black. He was asked by Mr. Gantz, "Did the hair sample found on the glove bear any characteristics similar to any particular race?" The answer was, "The hair maintained characteristics of the negro race in that it had a very black, very course texture."

Mr. Eltzeroth further testified that he had examined the gas can and nozzle for latent fingerprints. He stated, "The prints found failed to exhibit a sufficient number of characteristics to determine any identification."

He also examined for fingerprints a burned section of medical adhesive tape two inches wide and the knotted neckties found near the bodies. No prints were found.

The cross examination by Mr. Jones was brief.

Q. Now, Professor-can I call you Professor?

A. Certainly.

Q. Are you going to tell us that that hair you found on that glove belonged to David Roberts?

A. No, sir, that was not my testimony.

Q. I didn't think it was either. I just wanted to make sure there wasn't any misunderstanding. That's all I have of this witness. Thank you Professor.

The next witness was **Robert Forney**.

He testified that he was a medical doctor and Professor of Toxicology at the Indiana School of Medicine. He had examined blood samples of William and Elizabeth Harold taken at the autopsies. He found no carbon monoxide in the blood indicating that they were dead before the fire. He found no evidence of drugs. He found that the percent of alcohol in the blood of William Harold was consistent with two beers and the percent of alcohol in the blood of Elizabeth Harold was consistent with two ounces of whisky.

At the conclusion of this testimony I adjourned court for the day. I again allowed the jurors to separate and admonished them as I had at the conclusion of the first day.

I thanked the jurors and told them to return the next day, November 12, at 8 a.m.

The trial jurors still have heard no evidence connecting Roberts to the burglary, arson and murders. The next day's evidence would attempt to connect Roberts to the crimes.

I wondered why the hair sample from the glove found inside the Harold's living room near the front door was not compared to a hair sample from Roberts. This was before DNA but it could have been determined that Roberts' hair had many similar characteristics to the hair found on the glove. There was no evidence that a hair sample had been obtained from Roberts or if obtained and examined, what the results were.

CHAPTER SIXTEEN
The Trial-The State's Evidence Day 3
November 12, 1975

At 8 a.m. the next morning, November 12, 1975, the cast again assembled and further evidence was presented by the prosecutor.

Phillip Barrier and Rita Barrier were the first witnesses of the day.

They testified that they were good friends of the Harolds.

At approximately 8:30 in the evening of January 19, 1974, they stopped by the Harold house. They went inside and visited for a few minutes with William and Elizabeth Harold (Billy and Ann). They noticed no damage inside the house. They were familiar with the room partition and stated that it was intact and standing up. The Harold children, Marie and Jenny, were at William's brother's house.

The four of them then went to the Regency Drive-In Movie Theater in Franklin. Phillip Barrier was driving. After the movie they went to the Pizza Inn in Franklin. The boys split a pitcher of beer and the girls had cokes.

Then they went to Green Acres Tavern in Franklin and arrived at about 2 a.m. The boys had two beers apiece and the girls had one drink. They stayed there until about 2:45 a.m. They then drove to New Whiteland and picked up the Barrier children.

Then they drove to the Harold house. They arrived there at about 3 a.m. or a little after that. When they arrived at the Harold house the Harolds noticed that the porch light was not on. They had turned the porch light on earlier and when they left the light was on.

William Harold went to the front door and Elizabeth Harold drove away in her car to pick up their daughter Jenny.

That was the last time they saw William and Elizabeth Harold alive.

They further testified that William and Elizabeth "were getting along that night and were not arguing or fighting or anything like that."

There was no cross examination.

The next prosecution witnesses were **Delores Buress** and **Patti Buress Regent**, her now married daughter.

They testified that at the time of the murders they lived about half a block from the Harold house and that on the night of January 19, 1974, they had seen a goldish big car which was between a '68 and '73 Buick, strange to the neighborhood, parked right across the street from their house at 11 p.m. and also at about 2:15 a.m. the next morning. There was a street light right next to the car. The car was facing away from the Harold house.

They said that cars were never parked where the goldish car was parked unless they were coming to their house.

The car was gone when they were awakened at 4:30 a.m. by the fire truck sirens.

When shown a photograph of Roberts' car Delores Buress stated that she did not get a good look at the goldish car and Patti Regent said, "I couldn't identify it positive."

Upon cross examination they stated that they had not seen anyone in or near the car.

Cindy Jenner, a teenage neighbor of the Harolds, testified next.

She stated that she often babysat for the Harolds and that on January 19, 1974, she had babysat for them from 7 a.m. until they got home from work at 5:30 p.m. She also stated that the hall wall clock was working and kept accurate time.

Also while at the Harold home she received a telephone call between two and four from a male concerning some sort of survey. The caller wanted to know if the Harolds were home and if not, when he could talk to them. She told him that they would be home by six o'clock.

Cindy further testified that the Harolds returned home about 5:30 p.m. Later when being driven to a ballgame by her father at 8 p.m., she observed that the porch light was on at the Harold house. On her return home at about 12 a.m. the porch light was off, the hall light was on, and the curtains pulled in the den at the Harold house. She said that the Harolds usually turned the porch light on when they left the house and turned the internal lights off.

Upon cross examination, Cindy stated that she had not seen anyone at or near the Harold house. She also stated that she could not identify the caller's voice as that of Roberts since she had never heard his voice.

During the testimony of the witnesses who lived in the Harold neighborhood, I made a time line on my yellow note pad as to when the gold car was seen, when the porch light was on or off, and when the Harolds were home. The time line was:

January 19, 1974

7-8 p.m. No parked gold car

8 p.m. Porch light on

8:30 p.m. Harolds leave home-porch light left on

11 p.m. Parked gold car seen

January 20, 1974

12 a.m. Lights on in den and porch light off

2:15 a.m. Parked gold car seen

3-3:15 a.m. Harolds arrive home-porch light off

3:15 a.m. Elizabeth Harold returns home with Jenny

4 a.m. Clock stopped from fire

4:30 a.m. Fire observed at Harold house-gold car gone

From the above time line it appeared that the driver of the gold car could have been parked near the Harold house, observing or at the Harold house from 11 p.m. until 4 a.m. Perhaps the driver left for awhile and was at the Waffle House between 1-2 a.m. looking for the Harolds (as testified to later by Terry Harold) and then returned. All three Harolds were in the house from about 3 a.m. until their deaths which, as to William and Elizabeth, was no later than about 4 a.m.

Winfred "Buddy" Harold next testified.

95

He testified that he was the brother of William Harold. He stated that that he was the operator of a Standard gas station located at the intersection of U.S. 31 and Main in New Whiteland. The station was about one mile from William Harold's house.

He stated that on January 19, 1974, he had three employees, his two brothers Terry Harold and Elijah "Junior" Harold, and Joe Moore.

He further testified that in the late afternoon of January 19th at about 6 p.m. a black male in his late 20s purchased $1.00 worth of gasoline for his car from attendant Joe Marcos Moore, 17. He stated that the male had medium black skin, a medium afro haircut, a medium mustache, long sideburns, and wore a black leather jacket. He was driving a 1969 or 1970 tan and gold Buick Riviera. The car had no hubcaps and the driver side skirt was missing.

Winfred Harold later viewed several automobiles at the Indiana State Police Post and testified that after looking at the 1970 Buick registered to David James Roberts that the car was the one, or identical to the one he had seen at his gas station on the 19th.

He was asked by the prosecutor if the defendant, David James Roberts, sitting at the defense table, was the person who had purchased the gas. Harold said he did not know.

Before cross examination of Winfred Harold, pursuant to the Motion in Limine, and before me, Winfred was examined under oath by defense counsel out of the presence of the jury concerning his alleged theft of Harold estate and guardianship funds. I ruled that there was not creditable evidence of any such theft and that such matter could not be raised by defense counsel upon cross examination.

Upon cross examination Winfred stated again that he could not now identify the defendant as the person who had purchased the gas.

The defendant at the time of the trial had a short afro, no sideburns, no mustache and was thinner than he had been in January of 1974.

Terry Harold was the next witness. He stated that he was working at the Harold gas station at that time and verified Winfred Harold's testimony as to the description of the black person who had purchased the gas. He stated that the vehicle at the gas station was like the one he had seen at the State Police Post and registered to Roberts. He could not identify the defendant in the courtroom as the person who had been driving the gold Buick. He said he did not get a really good look at the driver.

Terry Harold then continued his testimony. He stated that at between 1:00 a.m. and 2 a.m. on January 20th, the morning of the murders, he was at the New Whiteland Waffle House. Part of his direct testimony states:

Q. Did you notice anything unusual at the Waffle House?

A. Yeah, I was waiting for my bill and there was a guy came in and looked around and he left again.

Q. What did he look like?

A. He was colored and had a black leather coat on. He probably stood six feet. Maybe more. He looked like the fella that I saw at the gas station earlier.

Q. OK. What drew your attention to this man?

A. Well, you know-I thought it was awful strange for a colored guy to just come in there and look around and leave again. Well, I been goin' there for about three or four years now and that was strange-having some guy come in there, done that and just left. Also, there were no colored that lived in New Whiteland or came to the Waffle House.

Soon after the murders, Terry Harold was shown six photos of African-American males including Roberts and he stated that the photo of Roberts was "very close" to the person he had seen at the Waffle House.

Terry also testified that he had been at his brother William's house often and on many occasions had observed water left in the bath tub even though no one was taking a bath.

Elijah "Junior" Harold was the next witness.

He stated that he also was working at the Harold gas station at that time and verified Winfred Harold's testimony as to the description of the black person who had purchased the gas. His description of the car was the same given by Winfred and Terry Harold. The car had no hubcaps and a fender skirt was missing. He also had viewed vehicles at the State Police Post and testified that the car at the gas station looked the same as the one at the Police Post which was registered to Roberts. He could not identify the defendant in the court room as the person who had been driving the gold Buick.

He further stated that he was very close to his brother Billy and often stayed overnight with Billy and Ann. Billy and Ann were very close, got along very well and never had any arguments. Billy had been a paratrooper in Vietnam.

Upon cross examination of Winfred, Terry and Elijah Harold, they stated that they were not positive that the car was Roberts' car.

The prosecutor then called **Joe Moore** to the stand. His testimony is as follows:

DIRECT EXAMINATION BY MR. GANTZ:

Q. State your name please.

A. Joe Marcos Moore.

Q. Okay. And where do you live, sir?

A. New Whiteland, Indiana.

Q. How old are you now?

A. Eighteen.

Q. Are you in anyway related to the Harolds of New Whiteland?

A. No.

Q. Now, drawing your attention to January 20, 1974, were you working at the Harold Service Station that day?

A. Yes.

Q. Now, do you recall anything unusual that afternoon?

A. In what way?

Q. Did you see-ah-did you see any unusual cars?

A. No, not really.

Q. All right. Did you wait on any persons in a Buick automobile?

A. Yes.

Q. And do you recall any one sale in particular?

A. Yes, I do.

Q. All right. And when did this sale take place?

A. About 4 o'clock in the afternoon.

Q. Okay. Now, did you sell some gas to someone?

A. Yes, I did.

Q. And is that your job to sell gas?

A. Yes.

Q. Did you make a sale of gas to this customer?

A. A dollar's worth.

Q. What kind of gasoline was that?

A. Premium.

Q. Okay. And did you have an opportunity to look at this car?

A. Yes.

Q. And what was the appearance of this car?

A. You know-it didn't look-you know-in real good shape or anything.

Q. Did you have an opportunity to see the color of this automobile?

A. Yes. It was a brownish gold color with a vinyl top.

Q. And what kind of an automobile was this?

A. It was a Buick Riviera-about a '68 or '9.

Q. Did you have an opportunity to observe the driver of this automobile?

A. Not real close, no.

Q. Well, do you-is there anything at all that you can say as a description of this customer?

A. Just that he was a black man.

Q. Can you say if he was a large man or a small man.

A. Well, he never got out of the car-you know-but he didn't sit to the shoulder though-you know-just kinda-I'd say about 6' 1" or so-you know-the way he sat in the car.

Q. After the 20th did you have occasion to view any cars at the Indianapolis State Police Post?

A. Yes, I did.

Q. Did you individually?

A. Yes.

Q. And, did you see any cars that you recognized?

A. Maybe.

Q. And what car did you recognize?

99

A. A Buick Riviera.

Q. Well, Mr. Moore, was this the same Buick Riviera that you saw in the station the afternoon of January 19, 1974 that you put gas in?

A. I'm not sure. It probably was.

Q. Now, back to the gas station. How long did it take you to put gas in the car?

A. Not very long at all.

Q. Okay. And then what did you do when you put the gas in the car?

A. I put the cap back on and he gave me a dollar.

Q. Okay. Was that the end of the transaction?

A. No.

Q. Well, what else took place?

A. Well, after he gave me the dollar, he asked me if-

MR. JONES: Just a moment. I want to preserve my record on this. We object to any statements made by a third party declarant outside this courtroom and not subject to cross-examination. This is clearly hearsay.

THE COURT: Objection is overruled-you may answer.

Q. What took place at this time?

A. Well, he gave me a dollar and as I was walking back toward the building he asked me if I knew where Pine Drive was.

Q. And what did you tell him?

A. I just pointed that direction and gave him what streets to turn on.

Q. Is Pine Drive the same street that William and Elizabeth Harold lived on?

A. Yes it is.

MR. GANTZ: Thank you Mr. Moore. No further questions.

CROSS EXAMINATION BY MR. JONES:

Q. A few questions, Marcos. How was this man in the automobile dressed?

A. Ah-well, I don't remember of him having a tie, and I don't remember him being real sloppy-you know.

Q. Is it a safe statement to say that you really don't know at this point anything except he didn't have a coat and tie on?

A. Yes.

Q. Now think very carefully Marcos. Was the man who bought the gas the defendant David James Roberts?

A. I don't know. I did not get a good look at him.

MR. JONES: Okay, Marcos, that's all I have.

MR. GANTZ: No further questions.

At the conclusion of this testimony I adjourned the court for the day. I again allowed the jurors to separate and admonished them as I had at the conclusion of the first day.

I thanked the jurors and told them to return the next day, November 13, at 9 a.m.

The jurors have begun to hear some evidence possibly connecting Roberts to the burglary, arson and murders. A gold car was seen the evening and early morning of the murders parked very near the Harold house, a gold or tan 1970 Buick Riviera driven by a black man the late afternoon before the murders was at the Harold service station, the driver had asked directions to Pine Drive where the Harolds lived, and the car was like the one registered to David James Roberts. No witness could identify Roberts as the person who had asked directions to Pine Drive. The next day's evidence would attempt to further connect Roberts to the crimes and provide a possible motive.

Tom Jones and David talked briefly on the front steps of the courthouse. They were encouraged by the day's testimony.

CHAPTER SEVENTEEN
The Trial-The State's Evidence Day 4
November 13, 1975

At 9 a.m. on November 13, 1975, court was again called into session. All parties and counsel were present. Further evidence was presented by the prosecutor.

The first witness called to the stand was **Lt. Robert Allen** of the Indiana State Police. He was the chief investigating officer of the Harold murders.

Lt. Allen testified that he had interviewed Harold family members concerning the personal and business lives of William and Elizabeth Harold. He was advised that William Harold worked at an Indianapolis Sears Roebuck in the automotive department. On October 10, 1973, a scheduled day off for William Harold, he was called in to work for another sick employee. Further investigation revealed that on that day he sold and had installed three tires and some muffler work done on a car for a black male in his late 20s using the name Robert Johnson. The purchaser drove the car away without paying for the tires or muffler work. The purchaser was later picked out by William Harold from a series of photographs. The photograph was of David James Roberts.

The next witnesses were **Dale Fleetwood**, service manager at the Indianapolis Sears, and **Floyd Huckleberry**, assistant manager at Sears.

They testified that William Harold worked under their supervision and that they had an October 10, 1973 sales slip and work order signed by William Harold as the salesman which named a Robert Johnson as the purchaser for three tires and muffler work. The sales slip and work order contained the serial numbers of the tires, indicated that it was to be a cash transaction and that such work had been performed. At the end of the day the car keys had not been picked up, the purchase price had not been paid, and the car was gone.

They reported the apparent theft to the security officer at Sears, Jerry Quackenbush.

The sales slip and work order were then admitted into evidence and shown to the jury. The purchasers name was Robert Johnson of 3357 Meadows Court and the total was $320.88. The serial numbers of the tires and the fact that the vehicle was a tan '70 Buick was also shown.

The prosecutor called **Jerry Quackenbush** as the State's next witness.

He stated that in October of 1973 he was a security officer for Sears and Roebuck in Indianapolis and a police officer of the City of Indianapolis. He had eleven years experience in criminal investigation. He had participated in the investigation of a theft of tires on the 10th of October, 1973 at the Indianapolis Sears Roebuck automotive store and service station.

He stated that he was the officer who had shown several photographs to William Harold and that William Harold had picked out the photograph of David James Roberts as the person who had ordered the tires and muffler work.

Officer Quackenbush was then asked how he knew the person in the photograph was Roberts. He answered that he had found the identity "from police records." This answer took defense counsel by surprise and he immediately objected on the basis of hearsay and the best evidence rule (that the actual photographs should be shown at trial to the witness). I overruled the objections and allowed the answer to stand. The proper objection should have been that the answer "from police records" indicated that Roberts had a criminal record and that evidence of a defendant's past crime is highly prejudicial and inadmissible. At the omnibus hearing I had ordered the prosecutor and any of his witnesses not to refer to or mention anything that would indicate a previous criminal record of Roberts. Defense counsel was in a bind though. If he objected to the "from police records" statement by officer Quackenbush for the proper reason, he would just be emphasizing to the jury that there was a police record.

Officer Quackenbush also testified that he had checked out the address on the sales slip and no one had ever heard of Robert Johnson at that address. It was a false name and address.

He next was asked by the prosecutor:

Q. And what did you do next?

A. I went to the parole office to find out where Mr. Roberts lived and where he was employed.

MR. JONES: Your Honor, does-now wait a minute. No objection yet.

103

Again defense counsel was taken off guard. Pursuant to my previous order the witness should have been instructed by the prosecutor not to refer to any inquiry at "the parole office." This definitely would call to the attention of the jury that Roberts was on parole. This was highly prejudicial. A person is not on parole unless he has committed a serious felony. If Mr. Jones had objected, I would have immediately sustained the objection and would have instructed the jury to disregard the fact that officer Quackenbush had inquired at Roberts' parole office. A lot of good that would have done. Once the cat is out of the bag- - -.

Sometimes a police witness will try and help the prosecution by slipping something into their testimony. Probably in this case it was inadvertent. I assumed that officer Quackenbush had been instructed by Mr. Gantz not to make any statement which would indicate Roberts' previous record. I called the attorneys to the bench for a private conversation and told Mr. Gantz that, except if Roberts testified or except in phase two of the trial, if any prosecution witness ever again made any reference to the previous criminal record or parole of Roberts that it could lead to a mistrial if requested by the defense. I adjourned court for a few minutes so that Mr. Gantz again could privately instruct his witness concerning any reference to Roberts' criminal record or parole.

Officer Quackenbush then described going to Roberts' employer's office and viewing a bronze '70 Buick Riviera registered to David James Roberts. He compared the serial numbers on the three tires on the Buick to the serial numbers on the work order and they matched.

On October 19, 1973, he later arrested David James Roberts pursuant to a charge of misdemeanor larceny (theft) filed in the Indianapolis Municipal Court. If convicted, Roberts could be sentenced to one year in prison and fined $5,000.00. Roberts posted bond and was released from custody. After several trial date settings and continuances, the final trail date was set for February 8, 1974.

Officer Quackenbush then identified the defendant sitting in the courtroom as the same person he had arrested on the larceny charge.

The next witness prosecution witness was **Deidre Edwards**.

She testified that she was a Court Reporter and that on request of the attorney for David James Roberts, Harold Chavis, she reported a written sworn Deposition given by William Harold on January 15, 1974. Present at the Deposition were William Harold, the deponent, Harold Chavis, attorney for David James Roberts, and Joseph Karen, an intern with the Marion County Prosecutor's Office. In the Deposition, William Harold described the entire transaction concerning the theft of tires and positively identified David James Roberts as the person who had ordered the tires and muffler repair.

The Deposition was offered in evidence and defense counsel strongly objected. He claimed that defendant would have no opportunity at trial to cross examine William Harold as he was deceased. How could defendant show any racial bias of William Harold? How could he bring out that William Harold was not sure of the identification? How could he show that William Harold had not dealt with many black men and therefore was not good at identification of them? Were black faces confusing to him? How could he show that William Harold had a motive to make a quick identification in order to get his sales commission?

I overruled the objection and admitted the Deposition into evidence. The Deposition was then read to the jury by the prosecuting attorney.

Trial of David James Roberts was of course never held as the primary witness, William Harold, was murdered on January 20, 1974, five days after his deposition identifying Roberts and nineteen days before the final trial date.

The jury had now heard evidence concerning a possible motive for Roberts to kill William Harold, the sole witness against him in the theft charge. The jury also had heard testimony that Roberts was on parole. A theft conviction would violate Roberts' parole and possibly lead to the imposition of a prison term for parole violation in addition to whatever sentence would be imposed on the theft conviction.

105

The next witness called by the prosecution was Indiana State Police Lieutenant **Robert Allen**. He had testified before.

He stated that he was the chief investigating officer in the Harold murders and in that capacity had interviewed 41 residents who lived in the vicinity of 915 Pine Drive. He also prepared and distributed 1000 copies of a flyer in an attempt to locate the source of the gas can found at the scene. The flyers were distributed on January 26, 1974, to police departments in New Whiteland and Indianapolis.

As a result of the flyer, he received information concerning the sale of a similar gas can by the Renkite Shell gas station in Indianapolis on January 19, 1974, the afternoon before the murders. At the Shell station he interviewed the owner, Elwin Renkite, and two employees, William Hardy and Richard Roman.

A copy of the flyer was then admitted into evidence.

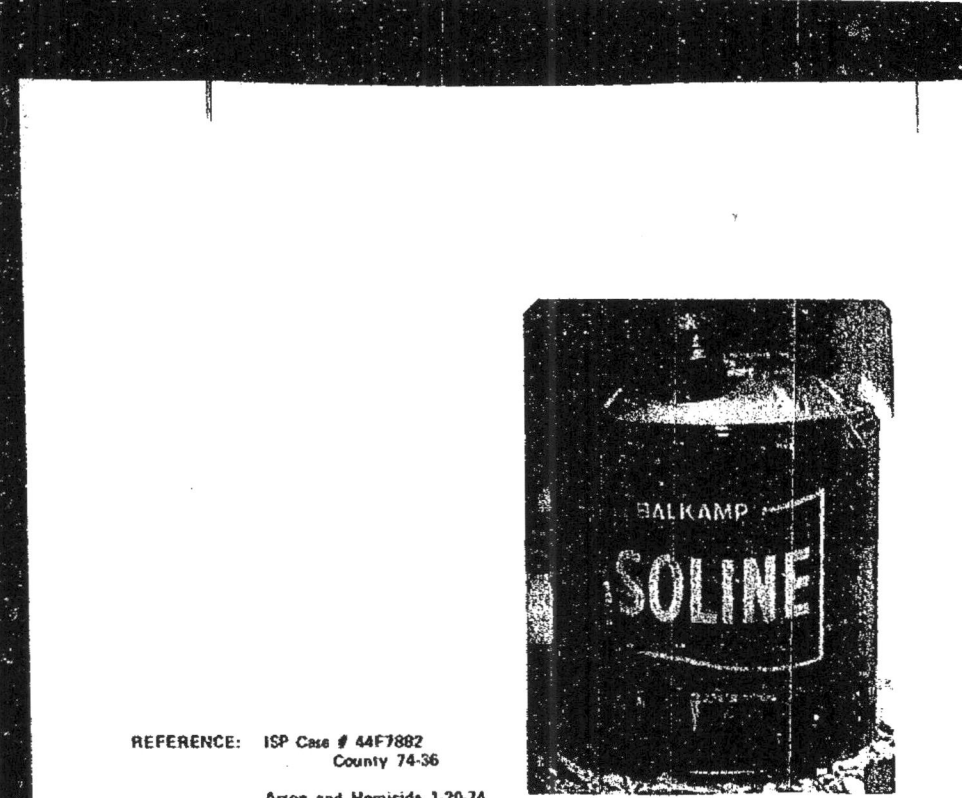

REFERENCE: ISP Case # 44F7882
County 74-36

Arson and Homicide 1-20-74

Attempt is being made to locate source of 5 gallon gasoline can at scene. Markings on can suggest it may be a "loan out" or "deposit" can.

Can pictured, replica of one in question and is as follows: Five 5 gallon capacity, red in color, with yellow word "GASOLINE" in approximately

2" letters. In smaller letters NAPA, Alcamp, Indiana USA. Stock # 14-1872, can has yellow plastic air valve, white plastic on handle and approximately 2 1/2" spout — bears yellow crayon markings on side: "$5.00 this can" Request checks be made with stations to determine if they are missing red, 5 gallon can — only in past two (2) months.

Any further information contact: Det/Sgt. R. L. Allen, Indiana State Police

107

Lt. Allen then stated that, pursuant to an arrest warrant, he had arrested David James Roberts on January 26, 1974, in Indianapolis and taken him to the Johnson County jail. Roberts had a pistol with him when arrested. Upon arrival at the jail Lt. Allen read the "Miranda Rights" to Roberts, allowed Roberts to read his rights, and asked him to sign the form acknowledging that he understood his rights. Roberts "Preferred Not to Sign" the form.

Lt. Allen further testified that at that time Roberts appeared to understand his rights, was not under the influence of drugs or alcohol and made no complaints of a medical nature.

Roberts did not request an attorney at that time and stated that he was willing to answer questions.

The Miranda Rights Form was admitted into evidence.

INTERROGATION; ADVICE OF RIGHTS

YOUR RIGHTS

Place _Ingalls, Ind IPP._
Date _11/26/74_
Time _5 00 PM_

Before we ask you any questions, you must understand your rights.

You have the right to remain silent.

Anything you say can be used against you in court.

You have the right to talk to a lawyer for advice before we ask you any questions and to have him with you during questioning.

If you cannot afford a lawyer, one will be appointed for you before any questioning if you wish.

If you decide to answer questions now without a lawyer present, you will still have the right to stop answering at any time. You also have the right to stop answering at any time until you talk to a lawyer.

WAIVER OF RIGHTS

I have read this statement of my rights and I understand what my rights are. I am willing to make a statement and answer questions. I do not want a lawyer at this time. I understand and know what I am doing. No promises or threats have been made to me and no pressure or coercion of any kind has been used against me.

Signed _Prefered Not to Sign._
DAVID JAMES ROBERTS

Witness: _R.L. Allen 1555_
Witness: _John Shauter_
Time: _5 00 PM_

#510A

STATE'S EXHIBIT #136

FILED
SEP 22 1976

CONTINUATION OF DIRECT EXAMINATION OF LT. ALLEN BY MR. GANTZ:

Q. And did you have conversations with Mr. Roberts after the reading of the rights?

A. Yes, sir.

Q. And what were those conversations?

A. I made inquiries as to his activities particularly on the dates of January 19th and January 20th, 1974. He answered that on January 19th at sometime between twelve noon and 1:00 p.m. he had went to Ayr-Way East, which is located in Indianapolis, and purchased points and plugs for an automobile. Then he purchased five or six dollars worth of gas at a Shell filling station across from Ayr-Way.

Q. Did you have other conversations?

A. Yes. I asked him what he did after 1:00 p.m. He advised he was working on an automobile behind the residence of Callie Loraine Myers, which is on Kingston Street, and behind her mother's house, at 604 Taft Road. Callie's mother's name was Florence Loraine. He worked on the car until the conclusion of the U.C.L.A. –Notre Dame basketball game.

Q. What other conversations took place?

A. I asked him who he might have talked to while at the residence. He said he had talked to Callie Myers, her brother LeRoy Loraine, and he had a brief conversation with her brother Dewey Loraine. I asked Roberts what he did after the ballgame and he said he left the Loraine residence to test drive his automobile. He said that at about 6:00 p.m. that evening he and LeRoy Loraine had went to Mandarin Inn, Indianapolis, a Chinese restaurant, and obtained some carryout food and returned to the Loraine residence where that food was consumed. I asked him who was present at that time and he stated that Callie Myers, Mrs. Florence Loraine, and LeRoy Loraine were present at the meal.

Q. Were there other conversations?

A. Yes. He said that after the meal he was at the Loraine residence watching television with LeRoy Loraine, and that at approximately 10:00 p.m. on that evening he went to Rudy's Liquor Store and purchased a half pint of vodka and some Colt 45, returning to the Loraine residence and watching TV and drinking those beverages with LeRoy until approximately 1:30 a.m.

Q. Were there any other conversations?

A. Yes, sir. I asked him his whereabouts after 1:30 a.m. He advised that he then returned to the Fall Creek Y.M.C.A where he was staying and upon arrival inquired of the switchboard operator if he had any calls. He then retired. He further stated that he arose the next morning at approximately 6:00 a.m., having went to sleep with the window open, awaking cold. He went out into the hallway and called the switchboard again inquiring if there had been any calls for him. He then went back to sleep until approximately 8:00 a.m. on the morning of the 20th. He said he dressed and proceeded to the Loraine residence and did have the noon meal at the Loraine residence.

Q. Were there any other conversations at that time which you recall?

A. Yes. I asked him if anyone else had used or borrowed his Buick Riviera over the weekend of the 19th and 20th. He stated that he was the only one to use the car.

Q. Any other statements by Mr. Roberts?

A. Yes, sir. Roberts asked what this was all about. There were conversations regarding the charges he had been arrested for, as to the location of the alleged crime, and as to who the victim was. There were conversations regarding a deposition which had been taken the proceeding week. I asked him if he was aware of the deposition being given, he answered, "Yes." I asked him if he was aware of the individual who had given the deposition and he referred to the individual several times as a fellow named Harris and once as Harold.

Q. Were there any other conversations?

A. Yes, sir, there were. David Roberts made the statement that, "I have not murdered anyone and I would be willing to take a polygraph on that particular subject matter." I advised him that it was unlikely that I could arrange a polygraph that particular evening and that if he was interested we could accommodate him on a polygraph.

Q. In the twenty-two months since that time has he or his attorney ever asked for a polygraph?

A. No, sir.

Q. Did you take certain mileage measurements?

A. Yes I did. The mileage from the Loraine residence to the Harold service station was 25 miles, from the Harold service station to the Harold house on Pine Drive was 1.1 miles, and from the Harold house to the Waffle House was .4 miles.

Q. Did you subsequently contact the Loraines and employees at the Fall Creek Y.M.C. A. to attempt to verify the statements of Roberts as to his whereabouts on the 19th and 20th of January, 1974.

A. Yes, sir, I did.

CROSS EXAMINATION BY MR. JONES:

Q. Lieutenant, in your interviews with the 41 residents on or near Pine Drive did anyone say that they had seen the defendant, David James Roberts at any time on January 19th or 20th, 1974?

A. No, sir.

Q. Now Lieutenant, as the chief investigating officer, how many gold or tan 1970 Buick Riviera automobiles did you find that are registered in Indiana?

A. I have no idea.

Q. Well then, how many in Marion County and Indianapolis?

A. We did not check that.

Q. Do you suppose that there are at least one hundred?

A. Probably not that many.

Q. OK, how about fifty?

A. I told you. We did not check.

Q. No. You did not check. Great police work Lieutenant. That's all I have of this witness.

RE-DIRECT EXAMINATION BY MR. GANTZ:

Q. How many gold and tan 1970 Buick Riviera automobiles with the hubcaps and a fender skirt missing are registered in Marion County?

A. I only know of one-Roberts'

There was no further direct or cross examination of this witness.

All of the previous witnesses were white. The next six witnesses will testify concerning their knowledge of the whereabouts of David James Roberts on the 19th and 20th of January, 1974. They were all African-American.

The next witness was **Florence Loraine**.

She testified that she lived on Taft Road in Indianapolis and that she had three children, Callie Loraine, LeRoy Loraine and Dewey Loraine. Her daughter Callie lived next door. She knew David James Roberts. Until about three or four days before January 19, 1974, he had been living at her daughter's house.

When asked if she saw Roberts on January 19, 1974, she replied, "Well, truthfully, I don't-I'm pretty sure that I saw him that day-you know. I don't remember what time I saw him that day or what he was doing." When asked if she saw Roberts on January 20, 1974, and was he there for a meal, she replied, "Yes, I did. I could not tell you exactly what time, but I saw him. He was not there for a meal."

The next witness, **Dewey Loraine**, stated that he had been to his mother's house briefly in the afternoon of January 19, 1974, and had seen Roberts there. He did not remember the exact time but he thought it was about 2:30 p.m. He did not see Roberts at any other time on January 19th or 20th.

The prosecutor then called **LeRoy Loraine** to the stand. According to the testimony of Lt. Allen, Roberts had told him that Roberts was at Florence Loraine's house watching television and having a few drinks with LeRoy Loraine from after dinner on the 19th until about 1:30 a.m. on the 20th, except for a brief trip to the liquor store at approximately 10 p.m.

LeRoy Loraine testified that he knew David James Roberts and that Roberts had been the boyfriend of his sister, Callie. He identified Roberts in the courtroom. LeRoy lived at his mother's house in January of 1974 and his fiancée was Veronica, his present wife. He saw Roberts working on his car in the back yard sometime in the morning of January 19, 1974. He also saw Roberts at his mother's house watching the U.C.L.A.-Notre Dame basketball game in the living room at about 2-3 p.m. He remembered having take-out Chinese dinner between 6-7 p.m. with Roberts, Florence, Callie and Veronica. After dinner he went into the den with Veronica and did not see Roberts again that evening. He thinks that Roberts left the house by the 10 o'clock news. LeRoy went to bed at about midnight and Roberts was not at the house. He stated that he had not been watching television and drinking with Roberts that evening. He had been with Veronica. He saw Roberts sometime on the 20th but could not remember when.

Upon cross examination LeRoy stated that he was not absolutely certain of the dates. He testified, "I am pretty sure. It has been twenty-two months ago, you know, but I do remember the basketball game and the Chinese takeout"

113

Veronica Loraine then testified.

She stated that she was at the Florence Loraine house the afternoon and evening of January 19, 1974, with her fiancé LeRoy. The only times that she remembered seeing Roberts at the house was when he was watching the basketball game at about 2 p.m. and when they all had Chinese food together at dinner. After dinner she and LeRoy were in the den and did not see Roberts after that. She and LeRoy came out of the den at about 11:30 p.m. to 12:30 a.m. and Roberts was not in the house.

The next witness was **Callie Loraine Myers**.

She testified that on January 19, 1974, she lived next door to her mother, Florence. She knew David James Roberts and identified him in the courtroom. She stated that Roberts was her boy friend and he had lived with her for about five months. He had moved to the Y.M.C.A. several days before the murders. The prosecutor asked her if she knew that Roberts had been married and had a small child. Callie appeared to be stunned. She whispered, "No". The prosecutor asked her to speak up so that the jury could hear. She said in a firm voice, "I don't believe it." Roberts had not told Callie that he had been married and had a one year old daughter.

Callie further testified that on January 19, 1974, she saw Roberts from noon until 3:15 when she noticed that his car was gone. She had watched the ballgame with him. She saw Roberts again between 5:30 and 6 p.m. at her mother's house and they ate Chinese later at about 6:30 p.m. with the family. She left her house to go out with a girl friend at 8:30 p.m. and that was the last time she saw Roberts that day or night. She returned to her house about 3 a.m. She saw Roberts at about 10 a.m. on the 20th.

On cross examination, she stated that Roberts had told her about the theft charge and "David was cool about it. He knew nothing was going to happen. He had passed a lie detector test and his attorney had told him that the case was going to be dismissed. He was not upset about the case at all."

She further stated that when she saw Roberts at about 10 a.m. on Sunday the 20th, "he acted normally and was not excited or upset. He was relatively calm. He was just like he was on all days."

114

The final witness of the day was **Juanita Richard**, the Fall Creek Y.M.C.A. desk clerk.

She testified that she had worked at the Fall Creek Y.M.C.A. for ten years and that she was the desk clerk. The desk clerk's duties were to "open the door and register anyone in if they come, and answer the telephone." Her hours were twelve at night until eight in the morning. Pursuant to the rules she always locked the only entrance door at twelve o'clock midnight and unlocked it between 5:30 and 6 a.m. The door was not locked during any other time of the day. She stated that she was employed and working her regular shift on January 19 and 20, 1974. She did not remember a David Roberts living there at the Y.M.C.A. Within a week after the murders she was shown a photograph of David James Roberts by a police officer and asked if she recognized that person. She said that she did not. She also was asked, "The picture that was shown to you, do you remember at that time whether you had left this person in between the hours of midnight and 6 a.m. on those dates?" Her answer was, "I don't think so."

Upon cross examination she stated that she was not positive that she had locked the door that night but she usually did because she was supposed to. It had been a long time age so she was not positive she worked those dates but she thought so.

She had stated that it was her duty to register anyone whom she let in. I wondered why the registry book was not offered into evidence.

At the conclusion of this testimony I adjourned court for the day. I again allowed the jurors to separate and admonished them as I had at the conclusion of the first day.

I thanked the jurors and told them to return the next day, November 14, at 9 a.m.

Today the jurors heard evidence that Roberts had been arrested on a Sears misdemeanor theft charge which was still pending when William Harold was murdered, that the sole witness who could identify Roberts as the tires purchaser was William Harold, that Roberts had been arrested on the Harold murder charges, that after his arrest he gave a voluntary statement to the police as to his whereabouts on January 19 and 20, 1974, and that important parts of his

115

statement were not verified and in some cases contradicted. The next day's evidence would be crucial to the prosecution. The prosecution would attempt to prove that in the late afternoon of January 19, 1974, Roberts had purchased the red five gallon gas can found in the Harold house. The prosecution had failed to do this at the bail hearing.

CHAPTER EIGHTEEN
The Trial-The State's Evidence Day 5
November 14, 1975

On November 14, 1975, at 9 a.m. the next morning the trial continued. Charles Gantz informed me and Tom Jones that the state's evidence would conclude that day. That would work out well as it was Friday and the court would be in recess over the weekend. The jury could rest up a little. On Monday, the defense could present evidence.

The next three witnesses were African-American.

The first witness called to the stand was **Elwin Renkite**. He stated that in January 1974, he was the owner of Renkite Shell Station at the corner of 16th Street and Meridian in Indianapolis. It was in an African-American neighborhood. At that time William Hardy and Richard Roman were his employees.

He further testified that he knew David James Roberts. He had been a good customer for over a year. Upon direct examination the following testimony was given.

Q. Do you think you could indentify him here in the courtroom?

A. I'm not real sure that I would-possibly.

Q. Well, is that person in the courtroom?

A. I wouldn't say yes. I would say possibly.

Q. You'd say possibly?

A. Possibly.

Q. And who might the person be who possibly could be David Roberts?

A. This man sitting here.

Q. Which man, sir?

A. The colored fellow right here-there. (The witness pointed to the defendant)

There was no further testimony from this witness.

William Hardy was next called as a witness for the prosecution.

He was about five feet two inches tall and very thin. He was the most nervous witness I had ever seen. His legs shook during his entire testimony. I had to ask him several times to speak louder.

William Hardy testified that he worked at the Renkite Shell Station at the corner of 16th and Meridian Streets in Indianapolis. That at between 5:30 and 6 p.m. on January 19, 1974, a black male in his late 20s, driving a 1970 tan and gold Buick Riviera, came to the Shell station. He stated that he washed the windshield of the car. The customer then purchased from Richard Roman, a fellow employee, some gas for the car. Also the customer obtained from Renkite Shell a five gallon red gas can with "$5 DEPOSIT ON THIS CAN" marked in yellow crayon on the side. At the customer's request, the can was filled with ethyl gasoline by Richard Roman. He stated that previously he, William Hardy, personally had written in yellow crayon "$5 DEPOSIT ON THIS CAN" and his name on the gas can.

He was shown the five gallon gas can found at the Harold house which had been previously admitted into evidence and identified it as the one loaned to the black customer. He stated that he could see his own handwriting on the can. He said that the gas can had never been returned to Renkite Shell.

He stated that he knew David James Roberts and that he had been a regular customer of Renkite Shell. He further testified that he recognized the defendant in the courtroom as David James Roberts but that he was thinner now, did not now have a mustache as he had before, and his afro haircut was longer then.

He stated that the vehicle being driven by the person who had purchased the gas for his car and obtained the gas can was exactly like the car that Roberts had always driven in the past.

He also stated that the man in the car was David James Roberts.

Cross examination and re-direct examination followed.

CROSS EXAMINATION BY MR. JONES:

Q. Mr. Hardy, is the Renkite station in a predominately black area?

A. Yes sir, right, yes, sir, about 9/8 of our customers is black.

Q. Now Mr. Hardy, do you remember being down in Johnson County and testifying in court at a bail hearing over a year ago?

A. Yeah.

Q. Now do you remember me asking you at that hearing if you would point out the man that borrowed that gas can from you on January 19, 1974? Do you remember that question?

A. Uh Huh.

Q. Do you remember that you were sworn by the judge to tell the truth?

A. Yes.

Q. And did you swear to tell the truth?

A. Yes.

Q. And do you remember tellin' the judge and me and everybody else in the world that the man who borrowed the gas can was not in the courtroom that day?

A. Yes, sir, I did.

Q. And isn't that the man that was in the courtroom that day? (pointing to the defendant David James Roberts)

A. Yes, sir.

Q. You know David James Roberts don't you?

A. I think I do.

Q. Is this the man that borrowed the gas can from you, or do you know?

A. I'm just gonna tell ya, I just don't know. I did not get a good look at him.

RE-DIRECT EXAMINATION BY MR. GANTZ:

Q. You testified that you had dealt with David James Roberts several times at the Renkite station.

A. Oh, yes, I have.

Q. Now, I want you to get down from the stand for a moment. I want you to get a good look and I want you to tell me-is this the man who got the red gas can from you recognizing the differences? (William Hardy left the witness box and stood right in front of the defendant) Is this David James Roberts right here? (the prosecutor points directly at Roberts)

A. It is.

Q. And that is the man that bought the can, is that correct, or got the can from the station?

A. Right, yes, correct.

FURTHER CROSS EXAMINATION BY MR. JONES:

Q. Well, now, didn't you just tell me this isn't the man?

A. I don't know-I'm all mixed up, man.

Q. Now, Mr. Hardy, David Roberts is on trial for first degree murder and it's becoming very evident that whoever purchased this gas can has a problem, and I want you to know, or want to ask you, sir, is this the man-can you say beyond a reasonable doubt that this is the man who purchased or got that gas can from you on January 19, 1974?

A. I just-I tell ya I just don't know.

There were no further questions by Mr. Gantz or Mr. Jones. The witness was excused. He hastily left the courtroom.

The next witness for the state was **Richard Roman**.

He stated that he was an employee of Renkite Shell on January 19, 1974, and his duties were to pump gas and run the wrecker. He testified as follows:

Q. Have you ever done business with David James Roberts?

A. Yes.

Q. Could you look around the courtroom and see if you could find this person that you know as David James Roberts?

A. I see-this fella looks like David Roberts-right here in the blue coat. (The witness points at the defendant)

Q. Now, sir, on January 19, 1974, did you have occasion to wait on David James Roberts?

A. Yes, sir, I did. I sold Mr. Roberts some gas for his car and in a can.

Q. What kind of an automobile was it he was driving?

A. It was a 1970 gold Buick Riviera.

Q. Did he have his own gas can?

A. No. We had a five gallon gas can that we had taken in and I let him have this can.

Q. Was there a deposit on this can?

A. Yes, sir. There was a $5.00 deposit on the can. He gave me his check for $5.00 as deposit and paid for all of the gas in cash.

Q. Was the check written on the 19th of January, 1974?

A. Yeah.

120

Q. Now sir, did you put gas in the gas can?

A. Yes. I filled it up.

Q. Did the gas can have a pour spout?

A. No. I got one off a two gallon can and put it on the five gallon can.

Q. And what did you do with the five gallon gas can?

A. I put it right down next to his car. Then I left to go and ring up the sale and that's the last time I seen the can.

Q. Do you know if that can ever returned to the station?

A. No, it didn't.

Q. I'll show you what has been marked as State's Exhibit #91 (the gas can found at the Harold house) and ask if you could recognize this can, sir?

A. Yes, I recognize the can as the one I gave to Mr. Roberts.

Q. You can recognize the can?

A. It's definitely the can.

Q. How do you know, sir?

A. It says "$5.00"-there is part of the "D"-deposit. It says "O-N (on) this". This is Bill Hardy's writin'.

Q. And this is the same can that you put next to Mr. Roberts' car?

A. Yes.

Q. Okay. Now, sir, you have testified at a previous bail hearing in Johnson County in which you failed to identify David James Roberts, is that correct?

A. Yes, sir.

Q. And does Mr. Roberts look different today than he did at that time?

A. Yes indeed. When I sold the gas to him he had a mustache, his haircut was a little fuller than what it is now, and he is slimmer now.

Q. Are you absolutely certain that this is David James Roberts (pointing to the defendant), the man that you sold the gas to, the man that got the can, the man that wrote you the check for $5.00 on January 19, 1974?

A. Yes, sir.

CROSS EXAMINATION BY MR. JONES:

121

Q. Now, let's get back to the bail hearing, Mr. Roman. At that time you told the court that it was not David Roberts that bought or borrowed a gas can from you-did you not say that?

A. Right.

Q. Your memory was fresh then, wasn't it.

A. I guess so.

Q. Were you sworn to tell the truth at the bail hearing?

A. Yes.

Q. Did you lie before God then or just now?

A. I have just told the truth. It was Roberts who got the can. I am not proud of my testimony at the bail hearing but I was scared to death. He had just murdered a witness against him.

Tom Jones jumped to his feet. "Objection, Your Honor. His answer was unresponsive and very prejudicial. I move the court to strike the last statement and admonish the jury not to consider it."

THE COURT: Objection sustained. The jury will not consider as evidence the last statement of the witness.

I could have admonished the jury by saying, "The jury will disregard and not consider the witness's last statement that Roberts had just murdered a witness against him." I cautiously did not do so. Some pro-prosecution judges would have.

Q. Now, Mr. Roman, could you be incorrect on the date of January 19th about the business about the gas can?

A. Could not be any other date.

There was no further direct or cross examination of Mr. Roman.

The State then called **Edward Sheets** as the next witness.

He testified that he was the Operations Manager at Midwest National Bank in Indianapolis. His position included having custody of bank records. He stated that David James Roberts had an account with his bank. At the request of the prosecutor he had brought accurate copies of all checks cleared by his bank written by David James Roberts for January and February 1974. He was asked if he had an exact copy of check number 205. He answered yes and produced the check.

The check was numbered 205 and was drawn on the Midwest National Bank of Indianapolis. It was dated January 19, 1974 and in the amount of Five Dollars. It was payable to the order of Renkite Shell. The check had DAVID J. ROBERTS printed on the top and was signed David J. Roberts. The check was offered and admitted into evidence.

The next witness for the prosecution was **Douglas Buck**. He stated that he was a Captain in the Indiana State Police and in charge of the Questioned Documents Section. He had over seventeen years experience examining and comparing handwriting.

He stated that he had examined check number 205 allegedly written by David James Roberts to Renkite Shell for $5.00 on January 19, 1974, and compared it with known exemplars of the writing of David James Roberts. Before he was asked to give his opinion, Mr. Jones on behalf of the defendant stipulated that the check was written by David James Roberts. The witness was thanked and excused.

Charles Gantz then called **Laurence Phillips** as the state's next witness.

Laurence Phillips stated that he was a detective sergeant with the Indiana State Police and that he was a crime scene reconstruction specialist. He testified as to his training and experience. He continued with his testimony as follows:

Q. Mr. Philllips, have you examined the exhibits introduced at this trial and read the investigation report prepared by Lieutenant Robert Allen, the chief investigating officer?

A. Yes, I have.

Q. And assuming that the materials and information that you have received are accurate, do you have an opinion as to what happened at the Harold residence in the morning of Sunday, January 20, 1974?

A. Yes, I do.

Q. And what is that opinion?

A. It is my opinion that William and Elizabeth Harold left their house at approximately 8:30 on Saturday, January 19, 1974, with their friends and returned at approximately 3 a.m. on January 20, 1974. William Harold went into the house. Elizabeth Harold left in the family car to pick up their daughter, Jenny, who was with a baby sitter. The murderer had probably been watching the house for some time and had sometime before midnight unscrewed the front porch light bulb to prevent being seen when he entered and left the house. After William Harold had gone into the house, the murderer then entered the house through the front door which was unlocked in anticipation of the return of Elizabeth Harold. The murderer was wearing leather gloves and may have hidden the gas can filled with gasoline outside the front door. William Harold then confronted the intruder and a struggle ensued in the living room and hallway. The intruder may have had a gun. William Harold was subdued and then strangled to death. His body was dragged into the den. Shortly thereafter, Elizabeth and Jenny returned to the house. The intruder hid until Jenny was placed in her crib. Then the intruder attacked Elizabeth and subdued her. Her wrists were bound with duct tape and her mouth was covered with duct tape. Her clothes had been removed. She was probably raped and then strangled to death with several men's ties fastened together. Her body was dragged into the den. The murderer then retrieved the gas can and placed it in the living room near the front door. He then removed the gas can spout, removed his gloves, placed matches on the floor and poured gas from near the front door to the den and on top of the bodies. Clothes from the nearby closet were piled on top of the bodies. At approximately 4 a.m. the fire started. I have no opinion as to why the gas can was left in the den and the gas can spout, matches and gloves were left near the front door. Perhaps the murderer then lighted the gasoline near the front door, watched as the flames followed the gas trail to the den, and then fled believing that the can, spout, matches and gloves would be burned and untraceable. The two to three gallons of gas found remaining in the gas can indicates that perhaps when the murderer was pouring gas onto the bodies gas vapor had spread to the pilot light of the gas hot water heater and a small explosion and subsequent flash fire erupted forcing him to immediately flee leaving the possible evidence behind. The front door was found open.

Q. Thank you detective Phillips. I have no further questions of this witness.

CROSS EXAMINATION BY MR. JONES:

Q. I just have a few questions detective. You were not there at the Harold house on that Saturday night or Sunday morning, were you?

A. No.

Q. You don't mean to tell the jury that the intruder was the defendant, David James Roberts, do you?

A. No.

Q. In fact you have no idea who the intruder was, do you?

A. I have no idea.

Q. You don't know really what happened, do you? It is just your guess.

A. It is my expert opinion based upon the evidence presented to me.

Q. Did Lieutenant Allen tell you about a black man named Douglas Milford driving slowly by the Harold house early that morning?

A. He may have mentioned that.

Q. Could Douglas Milford have been the person who murdered the Harolds?

A. I don't know. He could have been. Anybody could have been. As I said before, I do not know who was in the house.

Q. Just so the jury is not confused-you are not saying that David James Roberts murdered anyone, are you?

A. No I am not.

There was no additional direct or cross examination of this witness.

Mr. Gantz then stated that the prosecution had no further witnesses and the State rested its case.

At the conclusion of this testimony I adjourned the court for the day. I again allowed the jurors to separate and admonished them as I had at the conclusion of the first day.

I thanked the jurors and told them to return Monday, November 17, at 9 a.m. at which time the defendant would have the opportunity to present evidence in his defense.

At the conclusion of the state's case, the defendant filed a motion for a directed finding of not guilty based upon the theory that I as the judge, and as the "thirteenth juror", had the right to and should enter such a not guilty finding as there was not sufficient evidence to allow a conviction. I denied the motion.

CHAPTER NINETEEN
The Trial-The Defense Evidence Day 6
November 17, 1975

At 9 a.m. on Monday, November 17, 1975, the cast again assembled to hear the defense evidence.

The jurors had been very attentive throughout the trial and were eagerly awaiting the evidence of the defense. They were expecting the defendant to testify.

Tom Jones called **Harold Chavis** as the defense first witness.

He testified that he was Roberts' attorney in the misdemeanor tire theft case. At his suggestion Roberts had taken a polygraph test concerning the alleged theft and had passed. The examiner concluded that Roberts was telling the truth when he stated that he did not commit the theft. The polygraph test was admitted into evidence. In the polygraph test the examiner concluded that Roberts was truthful in stating that he had never purchased any tires from Sears.

Mr. Chavis further testified that even though the positive results of a polygraph test are not admissible in a criminal trial in Indiana to prove innocence, it had been his experience that in misdemeanor cases a positive result would lead to a dismissal of the charges. He was anticipating that the charges against Roberts would be dismissed. He told this to Roberts. However, the prosecutor was dragging his feet and had not yet agreed to a dismissal.

Mr. Chavis had then taken William Harold's deposition. Roberts was aware that the deposition had been taken and that the matter was still set for trial. He told Roberts that if the matter went to trial that it would be his word against Harold's and that he would argue that, "It doesn't make sense if a man's gonna steal some tires to let 'em get all of the information about the tire serial numbers and then steal the tires." He told Roberts, "But you know judges and juries do funny things so we better have you take a polygraph."

Mr. Chavis concluded his testimony as follows.

126

Q. Mr. Chavis, you stated that Mr. Roberts was aware of the trial date?

A. Correct.

Q. Had the case been set for trial before?

A. Yes. It had been set for trial two times before and then was continued.

Q. Nothing had happened to the prosecuting witness William Harold before these other prior settings? No witnesses were murdered before those trial dates, were they?

A. No.

Q. Have you had anything to do with the homicide case we are trying today.

A. Well, no. I think David called me at home. He had been arrested, upset, and he said something that he didn't understand what it was all about.

There was no further examination of this witness.

The defense did not offer any further evidence that Roberts was at the Y.M.C.A. at the time of the murders as set forth in his previous Alibi Notice. When he was arrested, Roberts had told the police that he was at the Y.M.C.A. and this was already in evidence.

The jurors anxiously awaited the next defense witness. They thought that it would probably be Roberts.

During the course of the trial, there had been many discussions between Tom Jones and Roberts as to whether Roberts should testify. Jones had explained that if Roberts testified, he would be under oath and must tell the truth. Also, Roberts had a prior conviction of a crime that would be brought out upon cross examination by the prosecutor. This conviction was relevant as to Roberts' truth and veracity. Once the evidence of the prior crime was introduced and allowed on cross examination of the defendant, evidence of Roberts' parole on this prior crime could be introduced by the prosecution. The possibility of a parole violation due to the tires theft could lead to additional time in prison. This would be an additional motive to murder Harold. Jones told Roberts that the jury would expect him to testify and explain why he was innocent of the theft and murders. The benefit of testifying would have to be weighed against the danger that the previous conviction and avoidance of additional imprisonment motive might influence the jury that he was guilty. Also, if he testified, the jury would expect Roberts to explain where he was on the evening and morning of the murders and why they should not believe that he borrowed the red gas can.

127

It is not known if Mr. Jones made any recommendation to Roberts as to whether he should testify. The ultimate decision was Roberts'.

I asked Mr. Jones to present his next witness.

Mr. Jones then stated that the defense had no further witnesses or evidence. Roberts would not testify. The jurors were startled. They wondered why he did not want to testify. Most jurors think an innocent person would want to testify.

There was no rebuttal evidence by the state. I admonished the jury and asked them to return November 18 for final instructions, closing statements of counsel, and deliberation.

CHAPTER TWENTY

The trial-Closing Statements and Final Instructions
November 18, 1975

On November 18, 1975, the attorneys for the parties gave closing arguments to the jury.

The prosecutor, Charles Gantz, addressed the jury first. He stood in front of the jurors and as he talked he looked directly at them and tried to make eye contact with each one. He meticulously described the events leading up to the murders which collectively could lead to only one conclusion by the jury that, beyond a reasonable doubt, David James Roberts murdered William and Elizabeth Ann Harold and caused the death of their infant daughter Jenny Harold.

He reviewed the theft charges against Roberts and the fact that Roberts might be sentenced to one year in prison and fined $5,000.00 if convicted of the theft charge. He stressed that William Harold had given his deposition one week before he was murdered identifying Roberts as the person who ordered the tires and that he was the sole witness against Roberts in the theft charge.

He stated, "It may be difficult for most people to imagine that anyone would murder to avoid a theft conviction. But Roberts is not a normal person. He does not think and act as you would. Look at the person who viciously strangled and burned William and Elizabeth Harold and you will see a person capable of anything. He had no regard for the infant Jenny. You heard the testimony of the crime scene specialist, Laurence Phillips. He told you what Roberts probably did inside the Harolds' house that terrible morning. Remember that Elizabeth was found naked. You can decide for yourselves what you think happened during that horrible hour before the murders."

OBJECTION BY MR. JONES:

I object to the last statements of Mr. Gantz. There was no evidence as to any rape and such a statement was only made to improperly inflame the jurors. The only witness that said anything about rape was the so called "crime scene specialist" detective Phillips and he was not there.

THE COURT: Overruled. You may proceed Mr. Gantz.

I overruled the objection because whether Elizabeth Harold had been raped was relevant on the issue of malice and premeditation necessary for first degree murder. The jury could infer from the evidence that Elizabeth had in fact been raped. Objections by counsel during closing statements are rare. They are often made to interrupt opposing counsel and divert the jurors' attention. A standard final instruction was given by me to the jury that the closing statements by counsel are not evidence but rather counsel's interpretation of the evidence.

Mr. Gantz continued, "The evidence clearly showed that on the afternoon before the Harold murders a black male about thirty years old driving a 1970 gold Buick Riviera automobile owned and registered to Roberts had asked at the Harold service station for directions to Pine Drive, the street on which the Harolds lived. Even though the witnesses at the Harold station did not get a good look at the driver and therefore could not identify the driver as Roberts, why would any black man in a white neighborhood driving Roberts' car, other than Roberts, have wanted directions to Pine Drive late in the afternoon before the murders? There was no evidence that any deliveries were expected by the Harolds."

Mr. Gantz took a brief look at his notes and continued, "The the red five gallon gas can found at the Harold house was obtained at the Renkite Shell Station in Indianapolis the afternoon before the murders by the defendant, David James Roberts. This evidence alone should convince you beyond a reasonable doubt that David James Roberts murdered the Harolds and set fire to them and their house. Richard Roman, the attendant at the Renkite Shell Station who knew Roberts as a long time customer, positively identified the defendant as the person who, late in the afternoon of January 19, 1974, drove into the station, obtained gas for his car, borrowed the red five gallon gas can, had the gas can filled with gas, paid cash for the gas, and gave his personal check for $5.00 dated January 19, 1974, as a deposit on the gas can. Roberts then drove away with the gas can. This was an African-American identifying another African-American."

"The writing on the red gas can was placed there previously in yellow crayon by William Hardy. Both William Hardy and Richard Roman stated that the car being driven by Roberts was a gold 1970 Buick Riviera which he had been driving for a long time" continued Mr. Gantz.

130

"Mr. Renkite and the two employees testified that the gas can never was returned to the Shell station."

Mr. Gantz stated, "It is understandable that William Hardy and Richard Roman did not identify Roberts at the bail hearing in Johnson County as the person obtaining the gas can. The survival rate of witnesses against Roberts before trial was extremely low. It took great courage for Richard Roman to now positively identify David James Roberts."

The prosecutor then said, "Remember that when questioned after his arrest, Roberts stated to Lt. Allen that he was the only one who ever drove his 1970 gold Buick Riviera."

There was a pause and Mr. Gantz looked at his notes again. He then said, "Roberts also stated to Lt. Allen that on the 19th and 20th of January, 1974, the night and morning of the murders, he was at the Loraine residence in Indianapolis and was watching television and having a few drinks with his girl friend's brother, LeRoy Loraine until 1:30 a.m. Roberts stated that he then left the Loraine residence and went to the Fall Creek Y.M.C.A. where he was then living. LeRoy Loraine stated that he had not seen Roberts after 7 p.m. and had definitely not been watching television with him that evening and early morning. Nobody at the Loraine residence had seen Roberts after 10 p.m. The Y.M.C.A. desk clerk testified that the only entrance door to the Y.M.C.A. had been locked by her from midnight until about 6 a.m. on January 20, 1974, and that she had let no one in during this period. Roberts had obviously lied to Lt. Allen as to his whereabouts the evening of the 19th and morning of the 20th. I'll tell you where he was. He was at the Harold house setting it on fire and maliciously murdering William, Elizabeth Ann and Jenny Harold."

Mr. Gantz walked to his table and took a small sip of water. He returned to face the jury and continued, "Roberts had motive, means and opportunity. There was understandably no witness to the murders and therefore technically no direct evidence. However, the circumstantial evidence is overwhelming and under Indiana law, a person can be convicted on solely circumstantial evidence as the judge will instruct you in his final instructions. I implore you, as the conscience of the community, to give closure to the Harold family and to render justice by reaching the only possible verdict-guilty on all counts. Thank you very much for your attention. Please do your duty."

The prosecutor returned to his table slowly. I turned to Tom Jones and said, "Mr. Jones, you may proceed."

Defense counsel, Tom Jones, then gave his closing argument. He also stood before the jury. He had a difficult challenge. He stated to the jury that it was hard to refute a suspicion of guilt raised by some of the testimony but suspicion was not sufficient to convict. Each juror must be convinced beyond a reasonable doubt of guilt.

No one saw Roberts at or near the Harold house. Were the identifications of Roberts and the car matters of honest but mistaken identity? Mistaken identity has been shown and documented in case after case. It is the leading cause of criminal convictions being set aside. No witness identified Roberts as the person who had asked for directions to Pine Drive at the Harold service station.

One witness at the Renkite Shell Station, William Hardy, had even cleaned the car's windshield. He knew Roberts well but could not identify Roberts at the bail hearing or at this trial as the person who had purchased the gas can found at the Harold house. Another witness at the Renkite Shell Station, Richard Roman, claimed to have loaned on deposit the five gallon gas can to Roberts. However, both William Hardy and Richard Roman when testifying under oath at the bail hearing in Johnson County shortly after the murders had failed to identify Roberts as the person who had purchased the gas can. Their memories of the events at the Renkite station were fresh then and they were under oath.

Defense counsel also asked the jury to consider whether William Harold mistakenly or perhaps purposely identified Roberts in the tires theft case? Why would a well educated and intelligent person such as Roberts commit such horrible crimes just to eliminate a possible misdemeanor conviction, especially since Roberts had passed a lie detector test and expected to be found not guilty?

Mr. Jones stated to the jury, "The police had completely failed to investigate other persons who might have committed the murders. They had their man. Why didn't the police find out

132

who had burglarized the Harold house and stolen clothes the week before? Why didn't they tell the jury why Douglas Milford was not a suspect? He was seen driving a car similar to Roberts' car in front of the Harold house early on the morning of the murders. He must have been connected to the murders and possibly committed them."

Tom Jones continued, "Roberts stated that he was at the Y.M.C.A. when the murders occurred. The Y.M.C.A. clerk was asked by the prosecutor if she let Roberts in the door that night or morning and she stated, 'I don't think so.' She appeared not to be certain and was hesitant when answering. She was not even sure of the date. She stated that she registered everyone who entered. Why didn't the prosecution obtain the registry and show it to the jury?"

Defense counsel explained that it was not the obligation of the defense to show that someone else might have committed the crimes. It was the obligation of the prosecutor to show beyond a reasonable doubt that it was Roberts and not someone else. He emphasized that the defendant was presumed innocent and that this presumption continued throughout the entire trial unless and until the state proved to each juror beyond a reasonable doubt each and every material allegation of the charges.

Defense counsel further stated that the filing of Indictments against defendant, as Judge Berger will instruct you, was not to be considered as any evidence of guilt as the Indictments were merely a technical way under Indiana law to commence a criminal prosecution.

He also explained to the jury, as the judge will also instruct you, that the failure of Roberts to testify on his own behalf cannot be construed by the jury in any way as an admission of guilt. He stated that the jury might understandably ask why if he was innocent he did not testify. He explained that there are many reasons why a defendant may choose not to testify: the defendant may be very nervous when testifying and his demeanor might imply that he was lying when in fact he was not; and the defendant may have been convicted of a prior unrelated crime which would be brought out by the prosecutor on cross examination, which prior crime may incorrectly influence a juror that the defendant was guilty.

133

Mr. Jones told the jurors to remember that even though David James Roberts had not testified, he had entered a plea of not guilty to all charges. This plea is equivalent to a statement by him that he did not commit the murders-that he did not borrow the gas can.

Mr. Jones stated to the jurors, "Your decision as to the guilt or innocence of David James Roberts is probably among the most difficult and important decisions that you will ever have to make. Do not forget the possible consequences of a guilty verdict. If you find Roberts guilty of murder in the first degree, then there will be a second phase to the trial. You will then hear further evidence about a prior crime and if you believe such further evidence has been proven, under Indiana law you will have to sentence David James Roberts to death. The prosecutor might prove such further evidence at phase two of the trial and therefore if you return a guilty verdict now of murder in the first degree you are actually sentencing Roberts to death."

Mr. Jones then explained that the judge would instruct them concerning the doctrine of lesser includable offenses. This doctrine states that if the jury is not convinced beyond a reasonable doubt that the defendant is guilty of first degree murder, then they may consider whether the defendant is guilty of murder in the second degree which calls for a life sentence rather than death, or a sentence for a term of years; or is guilty of voluntary manslaughter which calls for a sentence for a term of years; or is guilty of involuntary manslaughter which calls for a sentence for a term of years.

Mr. Jones also explained that Judge Berger will instruct them concerning the jury's right to determine the law and that they could disregard the law for a substantial reason. Mr. Jones stated, "Therefore if any juror has a substantial reason to believe that a certain law should not apply to this case, he or she may disregard the strict application of that law and render a decision that he or she believes is a fair and honest application of that law."

Mr. Jones declared to the jury, "You have heard five days of prosecution evidence. The only evidence that you have heard which connects David James Roberts to the crimes is the testimony of Richard Roman concerning the gas can loan. By his plea of not guilty, Roberts has denied that he borrowed any gas can. All the other evidence is 'maybe' or 'possibly' or 'I'm not sure' or 'could have been.' This is not the type of evidence which would allow a finding of guilt beyond a reasonable doubt. That leaves the jury with only the testimony of Roman. Remember, he testified under oath and before God at the bail hearing a few weeks after the crimes were committed that David James Roberts was definitely not the purchaser of the gas can. His memory was fresh then. Now over a year later he suddenly changes his mind. If you are not convinced beyond a reasonable doubt that Richard Roman has spoken the truth at this trial, then you must acquit David James Roberts. It all comes down to that. Ladies and gentlemen, I beg you not to find David James Roberts guilty of these crimes. A guilty decision would most likely result in a mandatory sentence of death."

Defense counsel ended by imploring the jurors not to be influenced by the type of crime committed or by sympathy for the Harold family. He stated that such feelings would be understandable but that the jurors had sworn to judge the facts without passion or prejudice, to faithfully apply the law as determined by them, and to render a fair and just verdict, not only to the State but also to David James Roberts.

Mr. Jones reminded the jury that Roberts was presumed innocent; that he had no burden to prove his innocence; and that the entire burden was upon the state to prove guilt. Further, he stated in conclusion that the state had failed to sustain such burden and that justice compelled the jury to find his client, David James Roberts, not guilty of all charged offenses.

At the conclusion of closing arguments, I read to the jury the court's Final Instructions which included most of the Preliminary Instructions with additional instructions concerning circumstantial evidence, the failure of defendant to testify, motive, lesser includable offenses, the duty of jurors to judge the law and the facts, and the filing of Indictments.

I further advised the jury that their sole function in this phase one of the trial was to determine guilt or innocence on all of the charges. I also advised that a finding of guilty on either Count I or III would result in a mandatory sentence of life imprisonment but that a finding of guilty on either Count II, III or VI would result in a mandatory sentence of life imprisonment and, under certain circumstances, death. The sentence on these counts would be decided by the jury at phase two of the trial to be held later if necessary. I further advised that a finding of guilty on Count VI would result in a mandatory sentence for an indeterminate term of five to twenty years.

Throughout the entire trial Roberts was always dressed in a dark suit and tie. He was always calm and attentive. He took notes and often conferred with Tom Jones.

After I gave the Final Instructions to the jury, the jury retired to the jury room to deliberate the fate of David James Roberts. A copy of the Final Instructions was given to the jury to consider during deliberations. It was 3 p.m. on November 18, 1975.

On the morning of November 18 while I was in my chambers preparing the final instructions, a member of the Indiana State Police spoke with me.

The officer stated that the Indiana State Police had heard from the Illinois State Police that a confidential informant in Chicago had heard a friend of Roberts, who had been a cell mate of Roberts, discussing plans with others to help Roberts escape if the jury should find him guilty of murder. The plans included possibly taking me or my wife and children as hostages to be exchanged for the release of Roberts.

The conspirators allegedly had made plans for Roberts to fly to Algeria which had no extradition treaty with the United States.

Roberts' brothers and friends were in Steuben County. Security at the courthouse was increased. I was advised to stay at the courthouse.

In response to the threat, I had my wife and two small children stay at the house of a friend. They stayed there until Roberts returned to Indianapolis the next day.

CHAPTER TWENTY-ONE

The Trial-Duty of Jury
November 18, 1975

There are two Indiana legal principles which give the jury great leeway in determining a proper verdict, "jury nullification" and "lesser included offenses."

JURY NULLIFICATION

I gave the following final instruction concerning the duty of a juror.

"DUTY OF JURY

In criminal cases the Constitution of Indiana gives the jury the right to determine the law as well as the facts. At the same time, it is my duty to instruct you concerning the law. This means that you should pay respectful attention to the law contained in my instructions, should give the law a fair and honest interpretation and should not ignore or disregard the law without a substantial reason. However, in reaching your final decision, you have the right to determine the law and the facts by which your verdict will be governed."

This instruction gave the jurors the right to determine the law and disregard it if they had a substantial reason. They could return any verdict they thought proper, even a not guilty verdict. What was a "substantial reason" had not been determined by the courts or legislature.

Jury nullification is defined as "A jury's refusal to apply the law because the result dictated by law is contrary to the jury's sense of justice, morality, or fairness." The Indiana Constitution in Article I, Sec. 19 states, "In all criminal cases, whatever, the jury shall have the right to determine the law and the facts." Does this provision to "determine the law" grant to Indiana juries the right of jury nullification? The answer is possibly "yes" until about 1983 and "no" thereafter.

137

This right to determine the law was first set forth in the original 1816 Indiana Constitution and was meant to give to the people a safeguard against oppressive government laws. This Constitutional right was incorporated in the 1851 Indiana Constitution and has never been repealed. Only two other states, Oregon and Georgia, have similar constitutional provisions. Does this Constitutional right to determine the law mean that the jury can under certain circumstances refuse to apply the law-to nullify the law? Even without a Constitutional provision, a jury always has the power (as contrasted with the right) to disregard the law and return a verdict of not guilty. A not guilty verdict cannot be overturned by a judge or court, jurors do not have to give any reason for their verdict, and the defendant cannot be tried again as this would be double jeopardy.

The above instruction which was given to the jury was based upon an instruction which was at that time approved by the Indiana Supreme Court. Today this instruction would not be approved. Later Indiana cases commencing in 1983 seem to state, without precedent, that a jury in determining the law can never disregard the law, even for a substantial reason! The Indiana Supreme Court by judicial fiat has in effect improperly repealed Article I, Sec. 19 of the Indiana Constitution.

LESSER INCLUDED OFFENSES

The doctrine of lesser included offenses can be described as follows. If a defendant is charged with "Killing another human being with premeditation and malice" as in the Roberts case the defendant is charged with First Degree Murder. By virtue of such a charge, under Indiana law, the defendant was automatically also charged with three other felonies. These are Second Degree Murder, Voluntary Manslaughter and Involuntary Manslaughter. Roberts could have been convicted of any one of these three lesser included offenses rather than First Degree Murder. I instructed the jury concerning this rule.

If the Roberts jury decided that Roberts did intentionally kill William and Elizabeth Harold with malice but did not plan in advance to kill them (no premeditation), then the jury could reach a verdict of Second Degree Murder and impose a life sentence or a definite sentence of from fifteen to twenty five years.

138

If the jury thought that such killing was done without malice and premeditation and "in the heat of passion," then the jury could reach a verdict of Voluntary Manslaughter which had a penalty of an indeterminate term of 2-14 years.

If the jury found that there was no intent to kill but that the deaths were the result of reckless and wanton conduct, the jury could reach a verdict of Involuntary Manslaughter which had a penalty of an indeterminate term of 1-10 years.

Defense counsel was relying heavily on these principles to avoid a conviction of First Degree Murder and the imposition of the death penalty. If one or more jurors were not convinced beyond a reasonable doubt of Roberts' guilt as to First Degree Murder or were hesitant to reach a verdict which would have required the death penalty, by using one or both of these principles, a compromise verdict could have been reached by finding Roberts guilty of Second Degree Murder or Manslaughter.

By using the above principles, juries can arrive at surprising verdicts from not guilty to a conviction of a lesser included offense. Most are "compromise verdicts." I presided over many trials in which I believe that the jury verdicts were based upon compromise or in some cases a complete disregard of the facts.

The following are three trials over which I presided which illustrate these principles.

TRIAL 1:

The defendant was charged with First Degree Murder: intentionally killing with malice and premeditation.

Defendant was very jealous of his wife and thought that she was having an affair with a fellow factory worker. At 11:30 p.m. the defendant's wife was returning home by car from work along a lane near their home. The defendant had been waiting for her and as she drove past him, he threw a large boulder at her car. She stopped the car and defendant ran up and opened her car door. He pulled her out of the car and slashed at her with a knife. She was able to spray him with pepper spray and ran down the lane away from the defendant. The defendant ran after her and repeatedly struck her with his knife in the back and finally in the throat which was fatal. He testified that he then lay on the ground, cradled her head on his lap, and began crying. He further

139

testified that he was afraid for his life as he thought she had a gun in her purse, and only stabbed his wife in self defense.

The jury reached a verdict of voluntary manslaughter. Some jurors thought that there was an intentional killing with malice and premeditation, and therefore murder. Some jurors thought that the killing was not planned, was done in the heat of passion, and therefore voluntary manslaughter. Some jurors thought that the killing was done in self defense. The final verdict appeared to be a compromise.

TRIAL 2:

The defendant was charged with First Degree Murder: intentionally killing with malice and premeditation.

The defendant and his wife often had heated arguments. During one such argument, defendant testified that his wife took a large kitchen knife and lashed out at him. As a result he received a small surface cut on his hand. He grabbed her and as they fell backward they broke a large ceramic jug. He picked up a jagged sharp piece of the broken jug and swung at his wife. According to his testimony, his wife stated that she was going to "kick him in the balls." Upon hearing this he stated that he had no choice but to immediately defend himself and his manhood. He stated that he took the knife away and stabbed her to protect himself.

The evidence disclosed that the defendant's wife had over thirty wounds on her body. Some wounds were caused by the knife and some by sharp pieces of the ceramic jug. Eleven deep wounds on the front of her hands and arms were described by an expert witness as defense wounds, those caused by holding out your arms to defend yourself.

The jury reached a verdict of battery and sentenced the defendant to six months in prison. Some jurors thought that there was an intentional killing with malice and premeditation, and therefore murder. Some jurors thought that the killing was not planned, was done in the heat of passion, and therefore voluntary manslaughter. Some jurors thought that the killing was done in self defense. The final verdict appeared to be a compromise.

TRIAL 3:

The defendant was charged with Rape.

The victims were two girls in their twenties who were on their way home to Boston from a vacation. They had been travelling in the western states and were hitchhiking along the Indiana

140

Toll Road. They were on summer vacation from a Boston College. While stopping at a toll plaza, they accepted a ride with a truck driver who was heading east.

An Indiana State Trooper was driving along the toll road and noticed a semi tractor trailer parked along the side of the road with the engine running. The trooper stopped to investigate and found the defendant and the two girls in the back sleeper portion of the tractor. One girl was huddled in the corner. The defendant was on top of the other girl engaged in intercourse. Both girls were crying. Both girls claimed that the defendant had beaten them and threatened them with further harm unless they allowed him to have intercourse with them. The defendant was arrested and charged with rape.

Within two hours the girls appeared before me to testify concerning their ordeal. The purpose of the hearing was to determine if there was probable cause to issue a formal arrest warrant. I found probable cause and issued the warrant. When the girls appeared in court they were still wearing their original clothes which appeared to be torn. Also many bruises were apparent to me.

The defendant appeared before me for preliminary hearing and bond was set. His trucking company posted bond. At the formal arraignment hearing, the defendant did not appear. I issued a warrant for his arrest.

The defendant was picked up for a traffic violation in Texas two years later. He waived extradition and was returned to Steuben County for trial. At that time it was not a crime in Indiana to "jump bail." The only penalty was to forfeit the bond which of course the trucking company had to pay.

The girls both returned to testify. The defendant testified that the girls had been pestering him for about fifty miles to stop and have some fun. Finally, being a normal man, he said he could not resist any longer and at their urgent request, he had intercourse with both of them.

The jury returned a verdict of not guilty! When asked why they returned a not guilty verdict, they stated that most of the jurors felt that any decent girl would not travel across the country hitch hiking and that if they did they "were just asking for it."

The defendants in the above three cases were wise to have a jury decide their cases rather than have it tried by the court (by me).

141

CHAPTER TWENTY-TWO
The Trial-Jury Deliberations
November 18, 1975

At 3 p.m. the twelve members of the jury entered the jury room to begin their deliberations. The alternate juror sat alone in the courtroom, admonished not to talk to anyone during deliberations. The door to the jury room was locked by the bailiff. The jurors would not be allowed to leave the jury room except for meals. At any meal they would eat together and apart from any other diners. As admonished by me, they were not to discuss the trial during any meal. They were in charge of the bailiff at all times.

The jury room contained a long rectangular oak table with turned legs and twelve oak ladder back chairs. There was no other furniture.

There was one picture hung on the wall. It was an old photograph of the first Steuben County jury that had women jurors. The year was 1936 and the photo showed eight women and four men, all with very serious expressions. The photograph also showed a young prosecuting attorney, Harris Hubbard, who was judge of the Circuit Court when I started law practice, and the judge at that time, the Hon. Clyde C. Carlin.

There were two rest rooms. The bailiff had provided a large pitcher of ice water and paper cups. Paper and pencils were available.

Under Indiana criminal trial procedure at that time, the jurors were not allowed to take notes during the trial. The jurors also at that time were not permitted to take exhibits with them into the jury room during deliberations. During deliberations, the jurors were not permitted to have a copy of the final instructions that had been read to them by me.

The reason for the rule against note taking as stated by the Indiana Supreme Court was to prevent the jury from being distracted by taking notes and perhaps missing some testimony.

142

The rule against having exhibits and instructions during deliberations was to prevent the jurors from giving extra consideration to one exhibit or instruction perhaps to the exclusion of others.

These rules completely ignored the intelligence of jurors and hindered their deliberations. I refused to follow the rule as to the exclusion of instructions from jury deliberations and sent a copy of the final instructions with the jury. Without the written instructions, how could jurors remember the eight essential elements of the murder charges against Roberts that they must find beyond a reasonable doubt to convict him? How should they reconcile contradictory evidence? What is a reasonable doubt?

In the Roberts case, the prosecutor and defense counsel did not object to sending a copy of the final instructions with the jury during deliberations. Defense counsel certainly should not have objected. It was to the defendant's advantage to have the jurors realize that there were eight essential elements which must be found to convict. Without the instructions as to the elements of each charge, the jury might remember only some of the essential elements and reach a wrong verdict!

In an appeal from a later murder trial over which I presided wherein I had again sent the final instructions with the jury during deliberations, defense counsel objected. The Indiana Supreme Court held that allowing the jury to have a copy of the final instructions was error. The Court stated however, that since the defendant had not shown how defendant was prejudiced by such action, the error was harmless and the conviction was affirmed.

In spite of the Indiana Supreme Court reprimand, I continued this practice in all civil and criminal cases.

Current Indiana Supreme Court Rules of Criminal Procedure now specifically allow note taking and the jury to have a copy of the final instructions and original exhibits with them during deliberation. Also a juror may submit a question to the judge to be answered by a witness.

After taking seats around the long table, the jurors first agreed upon a foreman. There were no volunteers and a well regarded farmer, Philip Michael, who lived on the family homestead near Fremont, Indiana, reluctantly agreed to be foreman.

All jurors agreed that the first thing that they had to decide was if the evidence proved beyond a reasonable doubt that David James Roberts intentionally killed William and Elizabeth Harold.

If they agreed that Roberts intentionally had killed them, then they would decide if the killing was done with malice and premeditation (Counts I and III).

They also had to decide if the deaths of William and Elizabeth Harold had occurred in connection with a burglary (Counts II and IV). Burglary required a finding of uninvited entry into the house by Roberts through a closed door or window and that he did so with the intent to commit arson, rape or murder.

The next decision for the jury was to decide if Roberts committed arson (Count VI) and if so, did such arson cause the death of Jenny Harold (Count V).

There was a general discussion by the jurors of the facts and the inferences that could be drawn. Some of the final instructions were reviewed.

The discussions were calm, deliberate and well organized.

Much weight was given to the possible identifications of Roberts' car at the New Whiteland and Indianapolis gas stations on the 19th of January, 1974; Roberts' statement to Lt. Allen that he, Roberts, was the only one who used or drove his gold 1970 Buick Riviera on the 19th and 20th; the testimony of Richard Roman wherein he positively identified Roberts as the person who obtained the red five gallon gas can from the Renkite Shell station on the 19th; the fact that the same gas can was found at the Harolds' house; the inquiry as to directions to Pine Drive, the street where the Harolds lived, by the driver of a car identified as Roberts' car; Roberts' motive to kill the sole witness against him on the theft charge to avoid conviction and possible imprisonment; the fact that the intruder did not take anything from the house (except possibly cash from the wallet and purse) indicating that the intruder was not a common burglar but had some other reason to enter the Harolds' house.

Several jurors remembered the statement that Roberts' parole officer was contacted. If Roberts was on parole, he must have been sentenced to a term of years for a felony and therefore would have to serve the remainder of the original sentence in prison as a result of any parole violation. This would add to the motive to avoid conviction on the theft charge.

144

The jurors also discussed the fact that Roberts had obviously lied to Lt. Allen as to his whereabouts on January 19 and 20, 1974. He was not with LeRoy Loraine watching television and drinking until 1:30 a.m. LeRoy Loraine was with his girl friend and not with Roberts.

Several jurors were concerned about a portion of the testimony of Lt. Lasiter. He stated that a fireman at the Harold house on the morning of the murders at about 6:30 a.m. had seen a car that looked like Roberts' 1970 Buick Riviera being driven by a black male. The fireman later was shown a group of photographs including Roberts' photograph. The fireman picked out a photograph of a person named Douglas Milford and not Roberts as the driver. Lt. Lasiter testified that he had investigated further and personally determined that Douglas Milford was not involved in the murders. The jurors wondered why the prosecution did not explain this further. Why did the police have a photograph of Douglas Milford? Why was Douglas Milford driving a car that looked like Roberts' car that early morning in front of the Harold house if he was not involved? What information did Lt. Lasiter obtain to lead him to believe that Milford was not involved in the murders? Defense counsel had probably brought out the Milford information on cross examination of Lt. Lasiter to raise the possibility that someone else other than Roberts was involved and possibly committed the murders. The jurors were concerned with this apparent lapse in the investigation.

After further lengthy discussions it was evident that all jurors thought that Roberts had planned to kill William and Elizabeth Harold, that he had killed them, and that he intended to kill them when he entered the house. The testimony of Richard Roman was crucial to the jurors. They believed that he had in fact given the red five gallon gas can to Roberts the afternoon before the murders.

As to Counts II and IV which required a finding of burglary and a "breaking" into the house, some jurors thought that there was no evidence as to how Roberts entered.

Since the jurors' verdict could result in the death sentence for Roberts, some jurors expressed the opinion that they could not make a mistake and if they were not absolutely sure, perhaps they should consider a verdict of second degree murder and impose a life sentence or perhaps a term of years from fifteen to twenty-five years.

The jurors decided to have dinner before further deliberations and so informed the bailiff.

After dinner the foreman asked each juror to express his or her opinion as to the guilt or innocence of Roberts. Ten of the jurors thought that Roberts was guilty on all charged counts. Two were hesitant. They said that they thought he was guilty but that since a guilty verdict could lead to a death sentence, they were reluctant to make such an important decision.

The jurors again reviewed the evidence. Further discussion followed.

The jurors decided to take a written secret vote. The jurors voted several times with further discussion after each vote. Finally, the vote was unanimous.

The foreman then knocked on the door and told the bailiff that they had reached a verdict.

All court personnel and the attorneys had stayed at or near the courtroom during all jury deliberations anxiously awaiting the verdicts. I was available at all times in case the jury had a question. There was a lot of nervous pacing. While the jury was deliberating, there was the usual speculation as to how long it would take for a jury decision. A fast verdict may or may not be a favorable one. If the jury took a long time to decide, perhaps they could not agree and there would be a "hung jury." If so, Roberts most certainly would be tried again or a plea bargain might be agreed to for a lesser offense.

CHAPTER TWENTY-THREE
The Trial-The Verdicts
November 18, 1975

At 8: 30 p.m. the jury indicated to the bailiff that they had arrived at their verdict. Roberts and counsel were advised and all returned to the courtroom.

The Bailiff led the jurors into the jury box. All was very quiet in the courtroom. The expressions on the faces of the jurors were somber.

I asked the foreman, Philip Michael, if the jury had reached a verdict and he answered that they had. The verdict was handed to the bailiff who then handed it to me. I read the verdicts to myself to see if they were in proper form. They were. I asked the defendant to stand and I read aloud the verdicts of the jury.

"We the jury find the defendant David James Roberts guilty of murder in the first degree as charged in Count I (intentional premeditated killing of William Harold with malice) and sentence him to life imprisonment.

We the jury find the defendant David James Roberts guilty of murder in the first degree as charged in Count III (intentional premeditated killing of Elizabeth Ann Harold with malice) and sentence him to life imprisonment.

We the jury find the defendant David James Roberts guilty of murder in the first degree as charged in Count II (taking the life of William Harold while committing burglary) the sentence to be determined after further evidence in phase two of the trial.

We the jury find the defendant David James Roberts guilty of murder in the first degree as charged in Count IV (taking the life of Elizabeth Ann Harold while committing burglary) the sentence to be determined after further evidence in phase two of the trial.

We the jury find the defendant David James Roberts guilty of first degree murder as charged in Count V (taking the life of Jenny Harold as a result of arson) the sentence to be determined after further evidence in phase two of the trial.

We the jury find the defendant David James Roberts guilty of arson in the first degree as charged in Count VI and sentence him to five to twenty years in prison."

Roberts showed no emotion. There was no celebration. All was quiet in the court room.

At the request of Tom Jones, the jury was individually polled by me. I asked each juror if the verdict of guilty on all counts was in fact his or her personal judgment. All answered quietly yes. I thanked the jurors and told them to return to court on December 3, 1975, at which time they would hear further evidence in order to determine if the death penalty would be imposed under counts II, IV and V.

I then issued an order that the defendant be held in custody without bail and delivered immediately to the Sheriff of Marion County, Indianapolis.

CHAPTER TWENTY-FOUR

Indianapolis

(Prior to Roberts' Trial)

On a frigid November night in 1974 a twenty year old white woman with her six month old son was driving her automobile in Indianapolis, Indiana, and stopped at a red light. Suddenly the passenger door was opened and a black male entered the car brandishing a handgun. He ordered the driver to drive to a vacant area on the outskirts of Indianapolis.

Upon arrival, he threatened to kill her if she resisted and raped her twice. She was then locked in the trunk. He drove the car several miles and then abandoned the car.

Later a passerby heard her pounding on the inside of the trunk and obtained her release. The infant was not in the car. The infant was later found dead at the side of a nearby roadway. The child had apparently been thrown from the car and died from exposure.

The police showed the woman several photographs of black males and she positively identified David James Roberts as her assailant. Charges of rape, kidnapping and murder were filed against Roberts in the Marion Superior Court in Indianapolis. He was immediately arrested and held without bail.

These charges were set forth in the newspaper article which some of the first panel of jurors had read which caused me to dismiss these jurors.

Understandably there was great condemnation in the press over the fact that, "a murderer had been released on bail by the judge to murder again." The Indiana Governor sent a special representative to Angola to question me as to why I released this murderer on bail. I explained to the representative that Roberts had been released on bail not by me but by the Johnson Circuit judge, and that considering the evidence at the bail hearing, the release was required by law. The

Governor's aid was not satisfied at all by the explanation and left stating something about liberal judges and that they were going to get that law changed. The law has not been changed.

Trial of these Indianapolis charges was held after the New Whiteland Roberts' murder trial in Steuben County ended. The first Indianapolis trial of Roberts ended in a mistrial. When the jury was deliberating, one of the jurors became ill and the deliberations could not continue. There was no alternate juror. A second trial was held and also ended in a mistrial. A juror during deliberations became mentally unstable and violent from the strain of the trial and had to be hospitalized. Again there was no alternate juror. The third trial ended with a conviction and sentencing of David James Roberts on all charges.

What courage the young woman must have had to testify in three trials.

CHAPTER TWENTY-FIVE

Roberts' Criminal Record

A criminal records check made before Roberts was charged with the Harold murders and arson revealed that Roberts had previously served about six years of a twelve year sentence at the Indiana State Reformatory for armed robbery in Crown Point, Indiana. The armed robbery occurred on March 11, 1966 when Roberts was twenty-two. The Amended Affidavit charging armed robbery stated that Roberts had obtained $1.50 from a woman by threat using a pistol. Roberts entered a plea of guilty pursuant to a plea bargain. The armed robbery statute called for a determinate sentence of between ten and twenty years. The Lake Criminal Court judge sentenced Roberts to twelve years in prison pursuant to the plea agreement.

He was on parole at the time of the Harold murders. He had served about six years of the twelve year sentence.

He was involved in a 1969 disturbance at the prison during which one inmate was killed and forty six others injured. As a result of injuries sustained in the disturbance, Roberts spent about nine months in the hospital. Roberts and 12 other inmates filed a one million dollar civil suit against the State of Indiana alleging the use of excessive force by state employee prison guards.

At the omnibus hearing the defense counsel had filed a Motion in Limine asking me to forbid any reference to the armed robbery conviction and parole in the first phase of the trial unless Roberts testified. I had granted the motion.

The decision by me to not allow the prosecutor to introduce evidence of or refer to the armed robbery and parole (except for cross examination of defendant if he testified) was made by me as a cautionary matter to avoid error. The prosecutor made a strong argument that he should be able to introduce evidence of a possible parole violation which was very relevant on the issue of Roberts' motive to kill William Harold to avoid six more years in prison for probation violation.

I had to weigh this against the possible prejudice to Roberts if the jurors knew of a prior serious crime having been committed by Roberts.

If Roberts had testified, the previous conviction of armed robbery would have been admissible upon cross examination as proper impeachment testimony. When a person testifies, the witness places credibility of the witness in issue and having committed robbery (theft from the person) is considered relevant as to the witness's credibility. Defense counsel did not want to risk having the jury hear such evidence. Even though evidence of a prior crime should only be considered by the jury as evidence of truthfulness, a juror might let the conviction influence the decision as to guilt or innocence and defense counsel did not want to take this risk by having Roberts testify.

Evidence of the pending Indianapolis charges of murder, rape and kidnapping against Roberts was not admissible as these were only charges. Even if they were convictions, evidence of these convictions would not be admissible to prove that Roberts committed the prior New Whiteland murders or as evidence upon cross examination relating to his credibility. Under Indiana law conviction of rape, kidnapping and murder is not evidence that a witness is not telling the truth or that he committed a prior murder! At the omnibus hearing, pursuant to defendant's Motion in Limine, I had ordered the prosecution not to mention these charges.

When the jurors had been deliberating the guilt or innocence of Roberts they had no knowledge of the rape, kidnapping and murder charges pending against Roberts in Indianapolis or of his previous conviction, imprisonment and parole for armed robbery. The jurors did not know that a conviction on the theft charge would have resulted in revocation of parole and six additional years of imprisonment for Roberts. This would have been a much stronger motive than only avoiding a theft conviction.

CHAPTER TWENTY-SIX
The Trial Phase Two
December 3, 1975

On December 3, 1975, phase two of the trial was held. The twelve jurors and the alternate returned to the courtroom and were welcomed again by me.

All attorneys and David James Roberts were present. Roberts was wearing his usual suit and tie but was shackled at his wrists and ankles. Before the jury entered the courtroom, over the objection of the sheriff, I directed that Roberts be unshackled. I thought that it would be prejudicial to Roberts to appear shackled. The jury would wonder why.

I first gave additional Final Instructions to the jury concerning the following.

The sole issue for determination by the jury was whether David James Roberts had been convicted of robbery prior to the Harold murders. If he had not, the mandatory sentence on Counts II, IV and V was life imprisonment. If he had, the mandatory sentence was death on each of said counts. The prosecutor had the burden of proving beyond a reasonable doubt that the defendant David James Roberts was in fact the same David James Roberts who had previously been convicted of robbery.

At the request of the Tom Jones, I also gave the following final instruction to the jury:

"The Indiana Constitution states that cruel and unusual punishments shall not be inflicted. All penalties shall be proportional to the nature of the offense. The Indiana Constitution further provides that the Penal Code shall not be founded on vindictive justice."

In 1983 the Indiana Supreme Court decided that the above jury instruction should not be given to the jury. The court held that these constitutional provisions were merely limitations on the legislature when enacting criminal laws and that the jury should not be made aware of these provisions. The court stated without prior authority or citation, "These proposed instructions would have conveyed to the jury that it had the power of nullification, which clearly it does not under the law."

After a brief opening statement, the prosecutor first introduced and had admitted into evidence a certified record of the proceedings before the Lake Criminal Court on June 17, 1966, which included Amended Affidavit of Armed Robbery, Roberts' guilty plea, the judgment of the court that David James Roberts was guilty of armed robbery, the sentence of twelve years imprisonment in the Indiana Reformatory at Pendleton, Indiana, and the Pendleton Admission Summary. The record disclosed that Roberts was represented by attorney Max Cohen.

The Amended Affidavit stated:

"That David James Roberts on the 11th day of March, 1966, did forcibly and feloniously take from the person of Mildred Wiscolik, by violence and by putting her in fear, certain articles of value, to wit: $1.50 in money then and there being the personal property of Mildred Wiscolik while the said David James Roberts was armed with a pistol."

The Admission Summary at Pendleton Reformatory contained the following:

"INMATES STATEMENT:

At the time of my crime, I was by myself. I saw three ladies in a car, and approached them and told them 'this is a stick-up.' I took $40.00 and fled. I was apprehended six blocks from the scene of the crime by the police.

I was then taken to jail and questioned. I was not advised of my legal rights nor was I permitted to call my attorney. I was then transferred to the county jail, where I stayed for approximately 4 to 5 months. I then entered a plea of guilty, was sentenced and transferred to the Indiana Reformatory at Pendleton.

The above is a true and exact statement given without threat or promise."

The record further showed his parole on December 18, 1972, and Division of Parole Initial Interview. The Interview states:

"REMARKS:

On 12-19-72 this writer read and discussed the rules and regulations of parole with Roberts and Roberts stated that he was aware of his obligations.

154

Roberts is originally from New Jersey, however, his family now lives in the Gary, Indiana area. Roberts had been given permission to marry a Miss Maryanne Dully, and the two should be married by 12-29-72.

Roberts now owns a 1970 Riviera Buick which is properly licensed and insured.

TENTATIVE EVALUATION:

This writer anticipates a successful parole for David Roberts. The subject has no previous criminal record and apparently was a good inmate while at the DOC Work Release Center."

The first witness for the prosecution was **Daniel Orewiller**.

He stated that he was the Director of Classification at the Pendleton Reformatory and had been for seventeen years. He was custodian of records which included the Inmate's Registry Book, fingerprints of all inmates, and photographs of all inmates. He stated that the records showed a David James Roberts as an inmate pursuant to a conviction of Armed Robbery in Lake County, Indiana. The records further contained the fingerprints and photograph of David James Roberts. He stated that he was familiar with the inmate David James Roberts and that the defendant in the courtroom was the same identical person. The registry, fingerprints and photograph were introduced and admitted into evidence. The photograph introduced was as follows.

155

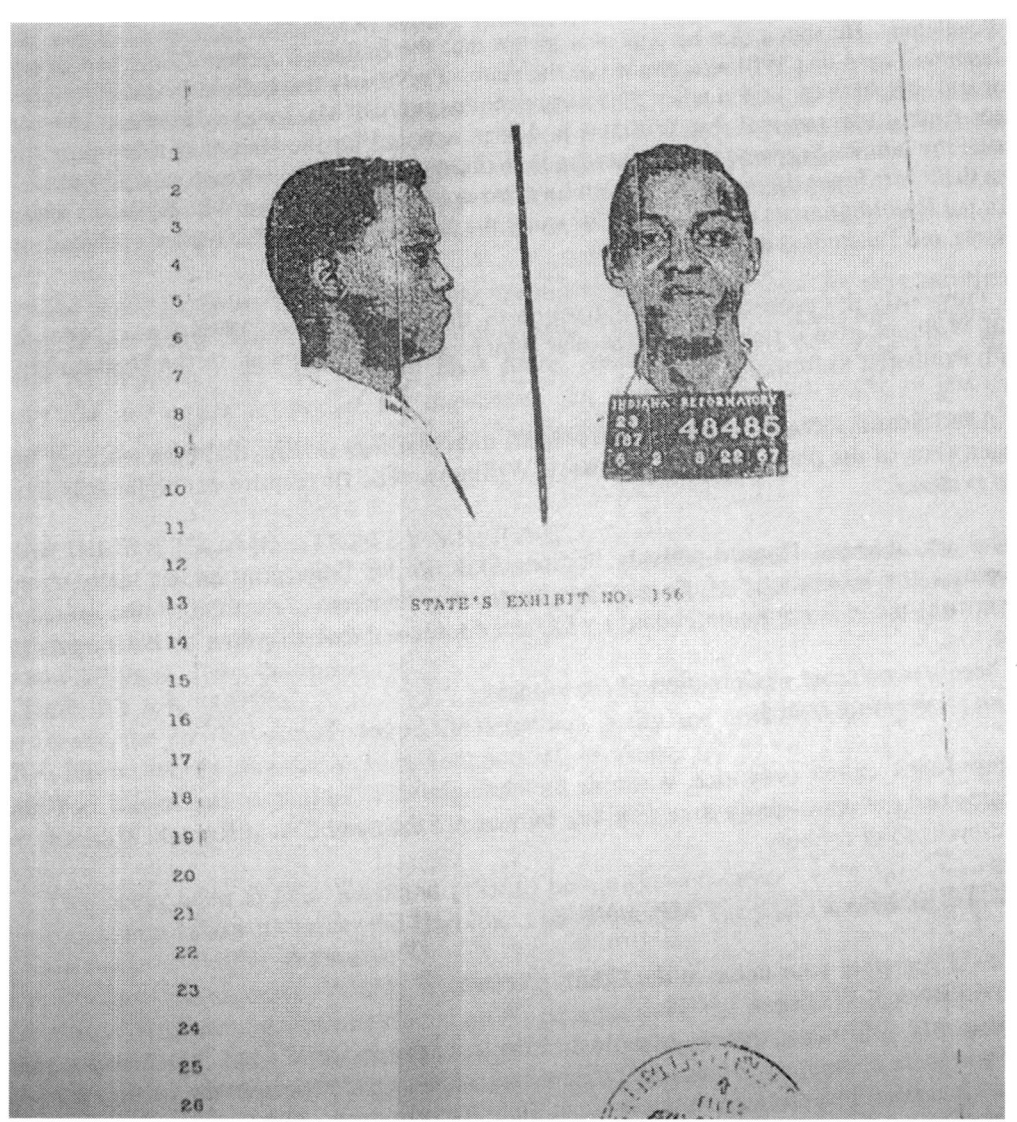

DAVID JAMES ROBERTS PHOTOGRAPH AT PENDLETON PRISON
AUGUST 22, 1967

Upon cross examination by Mr. Jones, the witness stated that he was aware of the law suit brought by the defendant against the State of Indiana for certain actions taken by guards at Pendleton. He stated that he was also aware that the Indiana Supreme Court had decided in a landmark case that Roberts could sue the state. Previously the Indiana law did not allow suits against the state for action taken place in prison by guards. Mr. Jones then asked the witness if he did not think it was unusual that Roberts had been arrested for the Harold murders just three days after the Indiana Supreme Court decision in Roberts' favor. The witness said he had no opinion on that. Mr. Jones then asked, "So you have no opinion as to whether Mr. Roberts was arrested for the Harold murders in retaliation for suing the State of Indiana?" There was objection by Mr. Gantz and I sustained the objection.

Previously the prosecutor, in anticipation of this penalty phase, obtained an order from me that Roberts give a fingerprint exemplar which could be compared to the fingerprints on file with Pendleton Reformatory.

Allen Stout, Indiana State Police Trooper, then testified that he had that morning taken the fingerprints of the defendant David James Roberts. The fingerprint exemplar was then introduced into evidence.

The next witness, **Donald Shively**, Indiana State Police fingerprint expert stated that he had compared the exemplars of fingerprints from the Pendleton records to the exemplars of fingerprints taken from the defendant by Officer Stout, and that all prints on both cards were the same.

There was no cross examination of the witness.

The prosecution then rested.

Tom Jones called only one witness: the defendant! The prosecutor could not object as Roberts had the opportunity to testify that he was not the same David James Roberts that had been convicted of robbery.

DIRECT EXAMINATION BY MR. JONES:

157

Q. Would you state your name to the Court, please?

A. David James Roberts.

Q. Now, Mr. Roberts, there's been testimony concerning an alleged "riot" at the prison in which you were apparently involved. Tell the jury what actually transpired.

A. Ah-I had been incarcerated in the Indiana State Reformatory. There was a disturbance on the opposite side of the reformatory. We were on a basketball court and we came around a corner and had a reformatory guard-several of them-level shotguns at me, and told me to lie down on my stomach. I was under the impression that this was to contain the masses-to have a mass arrest so to speak. This was not unusual. The crowd was orderly and they were obeying orders. It was quiet. I no sooner lay down on my stomach in a total surrender position-the guards were behind a cyclone fence-and for no apparent reason they opened fire on us repeatedly thirty-one times.

Q. Were you shot up in that incident?

A. I was shot five times and had my left arm almost severed.

Q. Now, did you require medical treatment over that-your arm and that sort of thing?

A. Yes, my arm and leg for approximately nine months in the Robert Long Hospital in Indianapolis.

In the heat of battle, sometimes really dumb questions are asked by counsel. This question is an example. Of course after being shot five times and having an arm almost severed, medical treatment would be required. It is like the old joke wherein a young reporter for a Washington newspaper asks Mrs. Lincoln, "Aside from the unfortunate incident with your husband, how did you enjoy the play?"

Q. Now did you file suit over this?

A. Yes, in federal and state court. The Indiana Supreme Court ruled for the first time that a prisoner could sue the State of Indiana for actions of guards-they handed down what is considered a landmark decision-I set a precedent in being allowed to sue the state.

Q. All right. Now when were you arrested for the offense down in New Whiteland?

158

A. Some three days after that decision was passed down. I think that they were out to get me.

All of the above questions and answers were not relevant to the sole issue for determination by the jury in this phase two of the trial. The sole issue was whether Roberts had a previous conviction for robbery. He had already been found guilty of murder in phase one. The prosecutor did not object to any of the questions. He probably did not want to possibly alienate the jury by objecting and appearing to limit the defendant in making his defense. He wanted to appear fair.

FURTHER DIRECT EXAMINATION BY MR. JONES:

Q. Now, I want to ask you, Mr. Roberts, one more question. Did you unlawfully and feloniously kill and murder anybody in New Whiteland, Indiana, on the 20th day of January, 1974 having then and there a prior unrelated conviction of the crime of robbery? I want you to look at the jury and tell them if you did that.

OBJECTION BY MR. GANTZ:

Your Honor, the jury has already found the defendant guilty and now he is trying to say he is not guilty. His answer is immaterial, irrelevant and self serving.

THE COURT: Objection overruled. You may answer, sir.

There was a hush in the courtroom. The jurors seemed to lean forward not to miss his testimony.

A. I-no, I've never been to New Whiteland prior to being arrested-never in my life. I swear to you before God that I did not murder the Harolds. I am innocent. I beg you to be merciful.

Roberts made no further statement.

The prosecutor did not cross examine Roberts.

There was no further evidence introduced by the defense or by the prosecution.

I told the jurors that they had now heard all of the evidence in this case and that they would now hear the closing statements of the prosecutor and the defense.

Mr. Gantz in his closing statement reminded the jury that the sole question for their determination was whether the defendant, David James Roberts, had a prior conviction of armed robbery or robbery. If so, they had a duty under the law to sentence the defendant to death. The evidence of his prior conviction was uncontroverted. The state had proved beyond a reasonable doubt, in fact beyond all doubt, that the David James Roberts who was convicted of armed robbery in the Lake County Criminal court was the same identical person as the defendant.

Mr. Jones in his closing argument reminded the jury that they were the judges of not only the facts but also of the law. "As you were instructed by Judge Berger, if any of you have a substantial reason to disregard the law, then you can do so. If there ever was a substantial reason to disregard the law, then this case is a perfect example. The evidence discloses that David Roberts was convicted of armed robbery based upon a charge of stealing one dollar and fifty cents! He was twenty-two and this was his first offense. He admitted to police that he had stolen forty dollars but he was only charged with stealing one dollar and fifty cents. To sentence David James Roberts to death for the theft of one dollar and fifty cents or even forty dollars is cruel and unusual punishment and is not proportional punishment. It is thereby forbidden by the United States Constitution and the Indiana Constitution. The Indiana Constitution specifically states that all punishments must be proportional to the offense and that the penal code shall not be founded on vindictive justice. You took an oath as a juror to render a fair verdict. The only fair verdict in this case is to disregard the harsh strict application of the law, which Judge Berger said you could, follow the Indiana Constitution, and determine that David James Roberts should not be sentenced to death based upon a charge and guilty plea of stealing $1.50. If you believe that the defendant has a prior unrelated robbery conviction, then the only fair verdict is to sentence the defendant to life imprisonment."

After these closing arguments, I read further instructions to the jury. The jury retired to deliberate.

After two hours of very serious deliberation, the jury returned their verdicts.

The jury sentenced David James Roberts to death on Counts II, IV and V.

Again there was no reaction from Roberts and the courtroom was quiet. The jury was again polled and all answered that it was their individual verdict that David James Roberts be put to death.

I have been unable to determine from the jurors I interviewed whether there was any discussion and sentiment by them concerning their right to "judge the law" and thereby refuse to impose the death sentence solely because Roberts as a twenty-two year old had been convicted of armed robbery of $1.50. Most probably, the circumstances of the crimes overrode any serious consideration of this aspect and, as one juror stated to me, "Three lovely lives were snuffed out for no reason. Why should Roberts have a life?"

The jury was thanked by me and excused from further service.

I then rendered Judgment of Conviction based upon the jury verdicts on all counts. I set the sentencing hearing for December 18, 1975.

I directed Thomas Hanselman, the probation officer, to prepare and file his pre-sentence report before that date.

Indiana law required a sentencing hearing and a pre-sentence report even though the sentences were mandatory. The jury verdicts of life, death and five to twenty years were not recommendations to me as judge which I could decide not to impose after a sentencing hearing. I had no discretion and had to enter the sentences found by the jury. In order to comply with the law however, I set and held such a sentencing hearing.

The sentencing hearing was held on December 18, 1975, with the defendant and all counsel present.

The pre-sentence report was filed by the probation officer.

In the report under "Offender's Version of Offense" it was stated, "The defendant told me, I didn't do it. I am innocent. I just can't believe all of this is happening to me."

The report also under "Present Attitude" stated, "The defendant's present attitude is very good. When I interviewed the defendant he answered my questions readily and without hesitation. He has the feeling that some people in some parts of the system are out to get him. He also told me that he was able to put it out of his mind. The defendant told me he has very few regrets. One of the things he wished he would have done was become a pilot, and at one time he would have liked to become a member of the Lake County Sheriff's department. The defendant

161

expressed the opinion that he could not see how the jury could have conscientiously returned their verdict."

Without hearing any further evidence or argument of counsel (Roberts declined to make any statement), I asked Roberts to stand and entered sentencing judgment as follows: "Mr. Roberts, pursuant to the verdict of the jury and Indiana law, I sentence you, David James Roberts, to life imprisonment on Count I (intentional premeditated killing of William Harold with malice); to life imprisonment on Count III (intentional premeditated killing of Elizabeth Ann Harold with malice); to death on Count II (taking the life of William Harold while committing burglary having committed an unrelated crime of robbery); to death on Count IV (taking the life of Elizabeth Ann Harold while committing burglary having committed an unrelated crime of robbery); to death on Count V (taking the life of Jenny Harold as a result of arson having committed an unrelated crime of robbery); and to five to twenty years imprisonment on Count VI (arson in the first degree)."

When I announced my sentences, I did not comment upon any aspect of the trial or direct any statement to Roberts. I had made it a practice not to address a defendant at a sentencing even when I had sentencing discretion (which I did not have in this case). Everyone knew the nature of the crimes and the effect it had upon the victims' family. Thoughts of rehabilitation were meaningless when the sentence was death. Most judges however at sentencing lecture a defendant as to how horrible his or her conduct was, how it had devastated the victim's family, how the punishment was justified and should be accepted by the defendant, and, if not a death sentence, that the defendant should work hard in prison to overcome his or her past. I do not believe that a judge should pontificate upon the obvious-that a judge should flaunt his seeming superiority of knowledge and morality. My motto was, "The less said the better."

I then entered an order staying the execution of the three sentences of death pending appeal to the Supreme Court of Indiana. The method of execution was by electric chair (changed to lethal injection in 1995).

The sheriff was directed to deliver the defendant to the Warden of the Indiana State Prison.

162

During the trial, except for determining whether there was sufficient evidence to avoid a directed finding of not guilty, I was not concerned with the guilt or innocence of Roberts. That was for the jury to decide. I was completely involved with making sure that the trial was fair and that no errors of law occurred. As I now reflect upon the evidence, I wonder how I would have decided if I had been on the jury. I believe that the evidence showed beyond a reasonable doubt that Roberts purchased the red gas can found at the scene of the murders and that he had a motive to murder to avoid imprisonment for the theft charge and possible parole violation. Who else except a person with a motive would have come into this quiet middle class white neighborhood and murdered the Harolds? But would I have been willing to find Roberts guilty of murder knowing that he could also be sentenced to death? I am very glad that I was not on the jury.

PART THREE

THE APPEAL

CHAPTER TWENTY-SEVEN

Motion to Correct Errors-Steuben Circuit Court
February 13, 1976

On February 13, 1976, the defendant filed a Motion to Correct Errors. One purpose of such a motion is to give the trial judge the opportunity to correct errors that he might have made at the trial and order a new trial if necessary. As you can imagine, not many of such motions were granted. Also, to preserve any objections for review by the appellate court, the objections had to be set forth in the motion.

The Roberts' motion set forth eight rulings at trial by me which were alleged to have been erroneous. It was also alleged that the evidence was insufficient to support Roberts' conviction. The motion also alleged that there was not sufficient evidence that Roberts had committed burglary, a necessary element of a conviction under Counts II and IV. The motion further alleged that the Indiana criminal statute under which Roberts was charged was in violation of the Eighth Amendment to the United States Constitution which prohibits cruel and unusual punishments as incorporated in the Fourteenth Amendment.

I directed the parties to file briefs concerning these matters and set hearing on the motion for March 11, 1976. After several continuances of the hearing date, hearing was finally held on June 14, 1976. Charles Gantz and Tom Jones were at the hearing. Legal arguments were made and I took the matter under advisement in order to review all of the legal citations and ponder my decision. I announced that I would render my decision on June 24, 1976.

I carefully read the relevant United States Supreme Court decisions cited by the attorneys. I had serious reservations about the constitutionality of the Indiana death sentence statute. One troublesome aspect of the statute was that it mandated a sentence of death for some murders and mandated a sentence of life imprisonment for other murders without any apparent rational reason for the distinction. As an example in the Roberts case a conviction under counts II, IV or V

167

mandated the death sentence for first degree murder if the defendant had an unrelated prior robbery conviction. However, the statute mandated that the penalty for first degree murder if the defendant had a prior unrelated first degree murder conviction was life imprisonment! If a defendant has committed a prior armed robbery the sentence must be death but if the defendant has previously murdered someone, the sentence must be life imprisonment! Determination of the penalty for a criminal offense is traditionally a matter to be determined by the legislature and courts defer to such determination. However such a distinction seemed manifestly unfair.

I was of the opinion that a more serious aspect of the Indiana death sentence statute was the fact that a mandatory death sentence as in the Roberts case did not leave any discretion with the jury to decide between a life sentence and a death sentence. Furman required, in determining a sentence of death, that there be a consideration by the jury of not only the circumstances of the crime but also the character of the defendant. I thought that mandating a death sentence does not allow for such consideration and therefore a statute mandating death may be unconstitutional as cruel and unusual punishment.

I took a brief vacation with my family to Sanibel Island, Florida, to try and relax after the emotional and mental strain of the trial. I especially wanted some quiet time to walk the beach to consider my decision on the death penalty. I was at that time personally opposed to the death penalty, and I did not want my personal opinion in any way to influence my legal opinion. In my mind I went over and over the reasons why I should or should not declare the Indiana death penalty statute unconstitutional. I remember on the last day of my vacation standing under the beautiful and rustic Sanibel Lighthouse and reaching my decision.

On June 24, 1976, I rendered my decision.

I first denied the objections to the eleven rulings that I had made at the trial, and I further determined that the evidence was sufficient for Roberts' conviction.

I then ruled that the Indiana death statute which mandated a sentence of death if the defendant had a prior unrelated robbery without giving the jury any discretion was unconstitutional as a violation of the Eighth Amendment prohibiting cruel and unusual punishments as incorporated in the Fourteenth Amendment to the United States Constitution.

I vacated the three death sentences I previously imposed under Counts II, IV and V and imposed life sentences thereon. I let stand the two life imprisonment sentences imposed under Counts I and III and the five to twenty years imprisonment under Count VI for Arson.

My decision to declare the Indiana mandatory death sentence statute unconstitutional and thereby vacate the death sentences, in effect agreed with and validated the argument of Tom Jones in the second phase of the trial. In the second phase, the jury had imposed a sentence of death rather than life imprisonment solely by virtue of a prior armed robbery of $1.50. The jury must have thought that a death sentence for armed robbery was not unreasonable, not unfair, not vindictive and not disproportionate. My decision basically overturned the jury's decision. The Indiana Constitution states in Article I, Sec. 18 that, "The penal code shall be founded on the principles of reformation and not vindictive justice." It is difficult to understand how electrocuting a person aids his reformation.

There were no Federal or State Court decisions which directly addressed this matter except a decision of the North Carolina Supreme Court which held that such mandatory sentences were constitutional. This decision was on appeal to the United States Supreme Court.

It is rare that a trial judge will declare any act of the Indiana legislature unconstitutional. The usual practice is to accept any such law and defer any constitutional challenge to the appellate courts. I felt strongly about this matter and was not willing to defer even though my decision would be contrary to the decision of the North Carolina Supreme Court.

The decision declaring the Indiana death penalty unconstitutional was not binding on any other court in Indiana and was subject to being reversed by the Indiana Supreme Court. The decision was not popular, except with the defendant, and some editorials were written strongly opposing the decision. I received several threatening anonymous letters. One stated that he hoped someone would burn my wife and children alive.

On July 2, 1976, eight days after my decision, the United States Supreme Court in *Woodson v. North Carolina* ruled unanimously that a mandatory death sentence was a violation of the Eighth and Fourteenth Amendments and ordered the Supreme Court of North Carolina to reverse the previous decision. The evidence disclosed that four armed men including Woodson, an African-American, drove to a convenience store. Woodson, who claimed that he had been forced to accompany the others, stayed in the car while two others went into the store. They shot the clerk and a customer, took the money from the cash register and fled in the car. The clerk died from her wounds. The jury found Woodson guilty of murder and sentenced him to death as required by the North Carolina statute.

It is interesting to note that at the time of the adoption of the Eighth Amendment, all states provided for mandatory death sentences for certain crimes.

By virtue of the *Woodson* decision of the United States Supreme Court, the Indiana death sentence statute, which was similar to the North Carolina statute, became unconstitutional. I was vindicated! To comply with the Woodson decision, the Indiana legislature in 1977 adopted a comprehensive new murder statute that provided for a bifurcated trial if the death sentence was a possible verdict, and set forth specific aggravating and mitigating circumstances which the jury must consider and find before a death sentence could be imposed. There are no more mandatory death sentences in the United States.

Except for death sentences, other felony mandatory sentences, such as life imprisonment without possibility of parole, are constitutional. A Michigan statute constitutionally requires such a mandatory sentence for possession of more than 650 grams of cocaine.

If the Roberts case had been tried under the new 1977 Indiana act, the jury would have been able at the sentencing phase to hear evidence concerning the Indianapolis rape, kidnapping and murder charges. The jury might very well have constitutionally sentenced David James Roberts to death.

CHAPTER TWENTY-EIGHT
Judicial Review

My decision to declare the Indiana death statute unconstitutional was the exercise of the power of a court (judicial branch of government) to declare the act of the Indiana legislature (legislative branch of government) void.

The Indiana and United States Constitutions create three seemingly co-equal branches of government (executive-legislative-judicial). The Constitutions do not specifically grant to the judiciary the power to review legislative or executive acts or action and declare them void. Where did I obtain such a power? The answer is John Marshall, third Chief Justice of the United States Supreme Court, who served for thirty-four years beginning in 1801.

The United States Supreme Court had an inauspicious beginning. Alexander Hamilton wrote in the *Federalist*, "The judiciary is beyond comparison the weakest of the three departments in power." The weakness of the early court was demonstrated by the fact that the new Capitol had not provided for a court room or chambers for the new Supreme Court. When the Court moved from New York to Washington in 1791, the Court held sessions in a plain room in the basement beneath the Senate Chambers. It was not until 1935 that the court would have its own building.

The perceived weakness of the court changed drastically when President John Adams appointed John Marshall in 1801 as Chief Justice at the age of forty-six.

Many contemporaries of John Marshall had serious doubts as to his ability to be Chief Justice. He was born in Fauquier County, Virginia, in 1755. He had very little formal education both generally and in the law. His formal education consisted of being schooled by a clergyman for one year and by a tutor who lived with the family for one year. The rest of his education was acquired from his father who himself had a very limited education. His legal education consisted of attendance at George Wythe's lectures at William and Mary College for six weeks.

171

George Wythe was a signer of the Declaration of Independence and a kindly and scholarly lawyer and jurist. In 1779, William and Mary College established a "professorship of Law and Police" and the Williamsburg institution appointed him to occupy the chair. It was the first law professorship in the United States. In 1806 he was tragically murdered by his grand-nephew. His grand-nephew, seemingly in debt and anxious to receive his legacy, poisoned Wythe's coffee. The testimony of the only witness, a cook, was inadmissible in Virginia because he was black, and the murderer was set free.

In 1818 the Indiana legislature passed an act excluding Negroes and Indians from testifying in courts of law in which any white person was a party in interest. The law was repealed in 1865.

In spite of such educational deficiencies, John Marshall during his tenure established the fundamental principles of the interpretation of the Constitution. Justice Oliver Wendell Holmes stated, "If American law were to be represented by a single figure, all would agree without dispute that the figure could be one alone, and that one, John Marshall."

In 1803 John Marshall rendered his famous decision in *Marbury v. Madison.* That decision established the doctrine that all actions of the legislative and executive branches of government are subject to review by the judicial branch and may be declared void if in violation of the Constitution.

Justice Marshall stated that although such power is not specifically stated in the Constitution, such power was necessary and inherent in establishing a constitution and a government pursuant thereto. He stated that the Constitution "confirms and strengthens the principle" of judicial review. Limitations on government power set forth in a constitution would be to no avail if no legal mechanism (the courts) was available to enforce them.

When I rendered my opinion on June 24, 1976, declaring the Indiana death statute unconstitutional, I was exercising the power of the court established by John Marshall 173 years before. If I had not done so, David James Roberts may have been put to death pursuant to an unconstitutional death statute.

CHAPTER TWENTY-NINE
Cruel and Unusual Punishments

The Eighth Amendment states, "Excessive bail shall not be required, nor excessive fines imposed, nor cruel and unusual punishments inflicted." The prohibition against cruel and unusual punishments was considered a basic right of the citizens and first appeared in the *Massachusetts' Body of Liberties* of 1641. Such a right was set forth in the federal Bill of Rights adopted in 1791 as the Eighth Amendment.

The prohibition against cruel and unusual punishments has two components. One component is that the actual punishments should not be cruel and unusual. They can be cruel if they are not unusual.

English and colonial history contain many cruel and unusual punishments. At one time using the rack, whipping, dunking or drowning in water, the shaming post, branding, cutting off ears, slitting noses, burying alive, beating to death and impalement were thought proper punishments. Treason was punished by first hanging, then cutting down while still alive, then disembowelment, then dismemberment. Such harsh and terrible punishments were never to be allowed again.

The second component is that the punishments shall be proportional to the offense. The Indiana Constitution states in Article 1, Section 16, "Cruel and unusual punishments shall not be inflicted. All penalties shall be proportioned to the nature of the offense." The concept of proportionality dates back to the Old Testament which proclaims "an eye for an eye" not an eye, ear and hand for an eye!

Imposing a mandatory death sentence in the Roberts case is an example of a violation of the proportionality component in the Eighth Amendment and the Indiana Constitution. The jury must have the opportunity not only to hear the facts of the crime but also any mitigating or aggravating circumstances before imposing the death sentence.

As noted in my opinion and the opinion of the United States Supreme Court, mandatory death sentences violated the United States Eighth Amendment prohibition against cruel and unusual punishments as incorporated in the Fourteenth Amendment. The "doctrine of incorporation" has a long and interesting constitutional history.

It is very important to recognize that the Bill of Rights (Amendments I-VIII) were prohibitions against federal government action. They do not impose limitations on state power (what a state can do). When the Bill of Rights was adopted, the citizens wanted to make sure that this new federal government that they had recently created did not infringe upon their rights. They were not concerned about any laws that their state might adopt and enforce. Therefore the Eighth Amendment did not prohibit a state from adopting and enforcing cruel and unusual punishments.

The Fourteenth Amendment was adopted in 1868. The original purpose of the adoption of the Thirteenth, Fourteenth and Fifteenth Amendments was to make the former slaves equal citizens. Such original purpose as to the Fourteenth Amendment has been drastically expanded by the United States Supreme Court.

The Fourteenth Amendment prohibits a state from acting (as contrasted with federal action). The Fourteenth Amendment does not specifically prohibit a state from imposing cruel and unusual punishments as the Eighth Amendment does. However, among the many prohibitions against state action contained in the Fourteenth Amendment are the words "nor shall any State deprive any person of life, liberty or property without due process of law." This is known as the "due process" clause.

The meaning of due process had a long and consistent history in England, the colonies and the United States. It meant that government must use a fair procedure before a person could be deprived of his life, liberty or property. A fair procedure included the right to be advised of the

174

charges against him and to be given an opportunity to defend such charges before an impartial tribunal. This later became known as "procedural due process."

As early as 1857 in *Dred Scott v. Sandford*, the United States Supreme Court incorporated a new concept into the meaning of due process. This new concept is called "substantive due process." The *Dred Scott* case held that taking property (slaves) away from the owner by legislation (the Missouri Compromise) was arbitrary and unjust, and if a law was arbitrary or unjust, it violated due process and was unconstitutional. This and subsequent decisions thus gave the judicial branch the right to inquire into all legislation to determine it was arbitrary or unjust.

Starting during the 1925-1950 period, the United States Supreme Court began incorporating within the due process clause another meaning never envisioned by the founding fathers. It was determined that there were certain "fundamental rights" which if denied by government would constitute a denial of substantive due process. What rights were a "fundamental right" and therefore protected against federal action by the Fifth Amendment due process clause and protected against state action by the Fourteenth Amendment due process clause would be determined on as case by case basis.

During this period, the Supreme Court determined that the prohibition against cruel and unusual punishments (federally prohibited by the Eighth Amendment) was a fundamental right and therefore incorporated in and protected by the due process clause of the Fourteenth Amendment.

During the period 1950-2013, the United States Supreme Court on a case by case basis ultimately incorporated all but four rights specified in the Bill of Rights into the fundamental rights concept. These four rights were not protected as to state action by the "substantive" due process clause in the Fourteenth Amendment.[13] Therefore by virtue of the Fourteenth Amendment all citizens are protected against a state taking action which violates the rights set forth in the first eight amendments except four. The four exceptions are (1) the Fifth Amendment right not to be prosecuted for a felony unless charged by a grand jury (as explained above the Roberts charges could have been brought by the prosecutor merely filing a criminal Information), (2) the Seventh Amendment right to a civil jury trial in all actions seeking $20.00

or more in damages, and (3) the Third Amendment right not to be forced to house soldiers in peacetime (which if ever claimed would be held to be a substantive right), and (4) the Eighth Amendment right prohibiting excessive fines.

It was not until 2010 that the Second Amendment right to bear arms was declared to be a substantive due process fundamental right protected against state action by the Fourteenth Amendment (McDonald v. Chicago).

Thus each state can begin a criminal prosecution by a criminal Information approved only by the prosecuting attorney and can deny or limit a jury in civil cases, all subject to the state's Constitution.

In addition to most of the first eight amendment rights being determined to be fundamental rights and therefore incorporated in the due process clause of the Fourteenth Amendment and binding upon the states, many other rights, based upon the values and view of justice held by the Founding Fathers applied to modern ever changing circumstances, have been determined to be protected fundamental rights. These include the "right to an habitable environment" and the very controversial "right to privacy" which has been determined by the United States Supreme Court to include the right to an abortion and the right to contraceptive information and usage.

CHAPTER THIRTY
Indiana Supreme Court Decision
May 5, 1978

The ruling on the Motion to Correct Errors was duly appealed, briefed and argued before the Indiana Supreme Court by prosecution and defense counsel. The prosecution did not appeal.

The Indiana Supreme Court consisted of five members. One member, Justice Roger DeBruler, had previously been judge of the Steuben Circuit Court and upon his appointment to the Supreme Court was succeeded by Judge Louis Sisler. Another member, Justice Richard Givan, was an Indiana Law School classmate and close friend of my previous law partner.

The Indiana Supreme Court opinion in *Roberts v. State of Indiana* was rendered on May 6, 1978. Justice Givan wrote the opinion of the court.

Several days after the Supreme Court decision was officially entered I received notice of the decision by mail. As I opened the envelope I nervously wondered- Had I been reversed? Had I made any mistakes in my rulings? Would the trial have to be held again? All of these thoughts came rushing through my mind. With trepidation I opened the envelope and slowly read the decision.

The trial court decision was affirmed.

The Indiana Supreme Court unanimously found that the evidence sustained the verdicts and that no error had been committed by me in my rulings at trial. The trial rulings were objected to on the basis of the best evidence rule, hearsay evidence being admitted (there were seven specific objections in this category), improper foundation being laid for the introduction of documentary evidence, inaccurate and inflammatory photographs being admitted and prejudicial questions being allowed.

The Indiana Supreme Court further affirmed the vacation of the death sentences and the imposition of three life sentences based upon Woodson and French. The court did however, by virtue of a recent decision, vacate the sentence of five to twenty years rendered upon the Count VI Arson conviction as being included in the life sentence rendered for the murder of Jenny Harold under Count V.

Justice Prentice agreed to the opinions of the other justices except that he dissented as to the guilty verdicts on Counts II and IV as these charges required a finding that the defendant had committed burglary. Burglary is defined as a breaking and entering with the intention of committing a felony. The Roberts' jury had also been concerned with this aspect. Justice Prentice believed that there was not sufficient evidence of a forceful "breaking" into the Harold house (if a person enters a house through an open window or door it is not a technical breaking). The other four justices believed that there was sufficient evidence of a breaking and stated in their opinion, "The Jury could have reasonably inferred from the evidence of a struggle inside the house and from the other facts leading up to the night in question that Roberts was not an invited guest of the Harolds and that his entry was attained by force."

In *French v. State of Indiana* decided on May 6, 1977, the Indiana Supreme Court formally struck down the Indiana 1973 death statute under which the Roberts case was tried based upon Woodson, thus effectively affirming my decision in Roberts.

It is interesting to note that in the *French* case the trial judge did not declare the Indiana mandatory death sentence unconstitutional as I did. The French trial judge upheld it and sentenced French to death. The majority opinion of the Indiana Supreme Court (who were elected at that time) stated, "Although the writer of this opinion does not agree with the present reasoning of the United States Supreme Court opinion upon the issue here involved, we have taken an oath to support the Constitution as interpreted by that Court. We have no alternative but to hold that the 1973 Indiana statute is unconstitutional." Justice DeBruler agreed completely with the reasoning of the United States Supreme Court. He did not pander to the electorate.

178

Tom Jones filed a Petition for Rehearing before the Indiana Supreme Court which was denied.

Roberts on his own behalf from prison obtained a complete transcript of the proceedings in anticipation of filing a Petition for Post Conviction Relief with the Steuben Circuit Court. Such a petition was never filed.

Roberts, still protesting his innocence and claiming that the system was out to get him, filed a Petition for Writ of Habeas Corpus with the United States District Court for the Northern District of Indiana. He claimed that his detention by state authorities was unlawful and wanted the federal judge to order his release. The District Judge denied his request.

There have been no further state or federal court proceedings.

CHAPTER THIRTY-ONE

Northwest of Indianapolis
October 25, 1986

On the morning of October 25, 1986, I was reading the Fort Wayne Journal Gazette and on the fifth page I saw a brief article with the headline MURDERER ESCAPES. I was in a hurry and almost skipped reading the article. Curiosity prevailed and I read it. David James Roberts had escaped from custody the previous day.

Roberts had been held since his convictions at the Indiana State Prison at Michigan City, Indiana, which is fifty miles east of Chicago, Illinois. The prison was built during the civil war to house Confederate prisoners. Three out of four of the two thousand prisoners were imprisoned for murder, making it one of the most dangerous prisons in the country.

Roberts had chronic lung problems and was often transported by prison guards from the Indiana State Prison to the Wishard Memorial Hospital in Indianapolis, Indiana, for treatment. Before leaving the hospital after treatment, Roberts was strip searched and shackled. When he was being transported back to the prison, a stop was made at a fast food restaurant. Roberts was allowed to go to the men's room. The guards stood outside. Upon leaving the rest room Roberts produced a .38 caliber handgun and ordered the guards to go to the parking lot. They all entered the police cruiser and a guard drove as directed to a nearby rest stop. At the rest stop Roberts forced the guards to unlock his shackles. The guards were handcuffed and Roberts went to a payphone. While Roberts was on the phone, the guards ran into the adjoining woods and escaped. Roberts then drove away in the cruiser heading northwest toward Illinois.

Obviously Roberts had help in his escape. Someone had to have placed the handgun in the men's room. Somehow Roberts had gotten the guards to stop at the right restaurant. The police speculated that one of Roberts' cellmates may have been his accomplice. The mystery was never solved. Both officers were subsequently disciplined for negligence in handling Roberts. One of the guards confessed to trafficking in contraband for prisoners and was summarily dismissed.

Roberts drove twenty-five miles to the next rest stop. A nondescript older car with the ignition keys under the front seat was waiting for him. He changed vehicles and drove north to the Indiana Toll Road and headed east toward New York City. The Indiana State Police alerted the police in the Gary and Chicago areas to be on the alert for Roberts. His family was closely watched.

Because of Roberts' history of revenge, the Indianapolis rape victim was moved by the police to an undisclosed location for a week. As a precautionary matter, the Angola City Police made extra patrols in my Angola neighborhood for several days.

Escape and kidnapping charges were filed against Roberts.

On April 27, 1987, Roberts was placed on the F.B.I. Most Wanted List.

CHAPTER THIRTY-TWO

America's Most Wanted

February 7, 1988

The first episode of the *America's Most Wanted* show, hosted by John Walsh on the new Fox Network, was aired February 7, 1988, seventeen months after the escape of David James Roberts. The first episode featured David James Roberts, his crimes and his escape. Although the program launched with the challenging statement "Watch Television-Capture Fugitives" no one knew if it would really work. Fox was a new network then, and *America's Most Wanted* showed only in a few areas.

Roberts was the only one featured that night, and as soon as the first commercial break started, the hotline began to receive calls. More than seventy-five calls were received. Most of the tips came from people in the New York City area.

One of the first calls to the hotline was from a woman in New York City claiming she was the girlfriend of a person named Bob Lord. She stated that she lived with him and that he showed a remarkable resemblance to David James Roberts.

She further stated that he had become ill and had gone to a hospital emergency room.

The New York City police and FBI immediately started their investigation. The woman identified Roberts as her boyfriend after being shown his photograph.

When authorities arrived at the hospital, they discovered that Roberts had suddenly checked out. When they went back to his room they discovered a copy of TV Guide laid on his bed opened to the story of David James Roberts on AMW.

Further investigation uncovered the fact that he was the director of a homeless shelter for men on Long Island and was known as Bob Lord. He had been earning an $18,000.00 annual salary. Everyone at the shelter was shocked. He was thought to be a friendly, caring and conscientious worker whom everyone liked.

Four days later on February 11, 1988, Roberts was captured without a struggle hiding out in an apartment in New York City.

Roberts was the first fugitive captured who was listed on the newly established F.B.I. Most Wanted List.

On January 27, 1989, Roberts plead guilty to escape and kidnapping, was sentenced, and was returned to the Indiana State Prison.

John Walsh interviewed Roberts after his capture. Roberts was asked how he felt after he had been profiled in the AMW show. Roberts stated that he was under great pressure. He knew he had to leave the New York area immediately. He did not know where to go. He could not go back to the Chicago area because the police would be looking for him there.

John Walsh asked Roberts, "How can you live with yourself knowing that you murdered two adults and two infants?" Roberts answered, "I can live with myself because I am not guilty of murdering anyone. Just because I was convicted does not mean that I am guilty."

Roberts further stated, "The *America's Most Wanted* program may have put persons who had not committed any crime back in prison. How do you feel about that, sir?" John Walsh did not answer.

Roberts then stated, "Mr. Walsh, I have had many despondent periods during my incarceration but I try to keep my spirits up. I constantly ask God why all this has happened to me. I hope that someday justice will at last prevail and someone out there will come forward with information that proves my innocence."

Thus ends, for now, the extraordinary tale of David James Roberts.

EPILOGUE

David James Roberts is currently serving four concurrent life sentences at the Pendleton Correctional Facility, Pendleton, Indiana. He is seventy-two years old. Roberts' civil law suit for damages against the Pendleton guards and the State of Indiana was ultimately settled. The amount of the settlement was confidential and not revealed.

Callie Loraine Myers, Roberts' girl friend, after the Roberts trial, attended law school, was graduated with honors and entered the practice of law. She later became a well respected judge presiding over non criminal matters.

Marie Harold was adopted by a loving aunt and uncle and has led a normal life. I recently received an email from Marie Harold as follows: "I just wanted to take this opportunity to thank you for writing the book, The Johnson County Murders. It was a little difficult at first to read with the pictures and details described in the book. You see, I am the surviving daughter and sister of the couple and baby who were murdered on January 20, 1974. The book answered many of my questions that family members could not talk about. I just wanted to thank you for speaking and writing the truth in regard to my family."

D. Charles Gantz founded Charles Gantz & Associates, a very successful law firm. He is still actively engaged in the general practice of law with emphasis on criminal defense.

Joe Van Valer founded the Van Valer Law Firm after his tenure as Prosecuting Attorney. It consisted of seven attorneys. He continued his successful legal career specializing in construction, real estate and corporate law until his death in January of 2011.

Tom Jones was the senior founding partner of the law firm of Jones, Auger and Auger. He specialized in criminal defense and personal injury law. He was the only Indiana lawyer listed each year since 1987 in the categories of criminal defense and personal injury in Best Lawyers in

185

America. He died on February 24, 2007 as the result of an automobile accident. The *Indianapolis Star* commented, "With the passing of attorney Tom Jones we lost a well liked and generous resident rooted in the history of Johnson County."

After I had served eight years on the bench as the sole judge of the Steuben Circuit Court, and having been the only judge in the county with general jurisdiction, I was exhausted both physically and mentally. I had begun as judge with high expectations of helping others resolve their problems and participating in the administration of justice. I was excited to take on the challenges. I was naïve. It did not take long before I was exposed to the raw underbelly of society. How could people act this way without any regard to others? I had never been exposed to or could imagine such actions. Persons appearing before me were murderers, rapists, burglars and thieves. Some defendants had committed incest, child abuse or domestic violence. Some were mentally ill, alcoholics or drug abusers. Married couples could no longer stand each other and could not wait to get a divorce. My actions and decisions as judge were necessary steps in the judicial process but I was wearing thin and it was taking its toll on me. I had given my best but after eight years "I had seen the elephant." It was time to move on and I resigned as judge.

After I retired from the bench I became Professor of Law at Tri-State University where I taught various law courses for twelve years. My wife of forty-two years, Susanna Ellen, died in 2005 of breast cancer. My two children live in Angola. I am now doing legal research, writing and lecturing in an attempt to help with the legal education of attorneys. I would like to be a good father and keep active as long as possible for, as in Robert Frost's insightful poem *Stopping by Woods on Snowy Evening:*

The woods are lovely, dark and deep.
But I have promises to keep,
And miles to go before I sleep,
And miles to go before I sleep.

The woods are lovely, dark and deep.

AUTHOR'S COMMENTS

The opening and closing statements of counsel at the trial were not recorded, were not a part of the official transcript and are therefore unavailable to me. Since I do not remember these statements after more than thirty years, I have taken the liberty of writing the statements as I would have made them if I had been the prosecutor and defense counsel. I hope that I have done them justice.

Since I was not privy to the jury deliberations, I have stated them as reported to me by two surviving jurors and the widow of the foreman.

The story portrays actual characters and facts. The trial testimony and exhibits are taken from the official Indiana Supreme Court 1400 page transcript.* I have changed the names of the victims and non police witnesses to protect their privacy.

* Detective Laurence Phillips, the crime scene reconstruction specialist who testified for the prosecution, is a figment of my imagination. I used his testimony to summarize some of the evidence and possible inferences. Most of his testimony, based upon proper objection, would have been inadmissible. An expert witness can only testify as to matters which an untrained layman juror would be unqualified to determine without enlightenment from an expert.

In my mind there were two troublesome questions remaining after the trial.

One was the twelve year imprisonment sentence that Roberts received for the 1966 Crown Point armed robbery of $1.50 in 1966. This seems excessive for a first offense. However, this sentence was the result of a plea bargain agreed to by Roberts. Why would Roberts agree to such a sentence?

Roberts explained the events to his Admissions Officer at Pendleton Reformatory as follows:

"At the time of my crime, I was by myself. I saw three ladies in a car, and approached them and told them: this is a stick-up. I took $40.00 and fled. I was apprehended six blocks from the scene of the crime by the police."

My recent search of the Lake County Superior Court records reveals a different story. There were actually five felony charges filed on March 15, 1966, against Roberts (involving two white women and a white man) including the original charge of Robbery ($1.50) from Mildred Wiscolik, which was changed by Amended Affidavit to Armed Robbery ($1.50) and to which

188

Roberts plead guilty; Inflicting Injury (striking, beating and wounding) Upon Mildred Wiscolik in the Perpetration of an Attempted Rape; Robbery of a ring ($300.00) and cash ($52.00) from Richard Lenoski; Kidnapping (forcibly kidnap, imprison and carry off) of Lynette Harnish; and Rape (forcibly ravish and carnally know) of Lynette Harnish. As a result of the plea bargain, the four additional charges were continued and Roberts plead guilty to an Amended Affidavit charging only armed robbery of $1.50. Because of the severity of Roberts' alleged actions and the possible total sentence on all five charges, the agreed to twelve year sentence seems reasonable. Roberts' attorney at that time, Max Cohen, recently stated to me that he thought that the sentence was fair and that Judge John McKenna usually set the terms of any plea agreement. The four additional charges were never tried and were dismissed on October 27, 1976 upon motion of the Lake County prosecuting attorney by virtue of the Steuben County and Marion County five life sentences. The Steuben County Roberts' jury was not aware of the Lake County four additional original charges during their deliberations.

The second question was the possible involvement of Douglas Milford who may have been seen driving near the Harold house the morning of the fire. Lieutenant John Lasiter, the Johnson County Deputy Sheriff who was a primary investigating officer, stated to me recently that the New Whiteland volunteer fireman who, according to his testimony, picked out the photograph of Douglas Milford as the "probable" driver of the large brown car the morning of the fire, was not certain at all of the identification. The fireman stated to Lieutenant Lasiter that of the six photos, the one of Milford most nearly resembled the driver. The fireman had little exposure to African-Americans. There were no African-Americans living or working in the area and unless a person worked with African-Americans routinely in Indianapolis or had other regular exposure to African-Americans (which he did not) he could not have identified a specific African-American with any degree of certainty. This is why Lieutenant Lasiter and Charles Gantz did not consider Milford as a suspect. It very well could have been Roberts checking to see the extent of the fire and if any evidence left behind was destroyed.

Lieutenant Lasiter also stated that he drove Roberts back and forth between Angola and Indianapolis during the trial. From the statements made by Roberts on these trips, Lasiter believed that Roberts was convinced that the white officers and prosecutors were out to get him and that he hated all whites. All of his victims had been white.

When I taught law at Tri-State University, I used the Roberts case as the framework to teach criminal and constitutional law and procedure.

The Roberts case was an excellent introduction to important procedural and substantive aspects of criminal law. It allowed me to illustrate how the United States Constitution is applied to an actual criminal case. The printed words of criminal statutes and the Constitution were brought to life. Words and phrases such as grand jury, murder, voluntary manslaughter, involuntary manslaughter, burglary, arson, arraignment, omnibus hearing, voir dire, jury instructions, death sentence, lesser included offenses, jury nullification, appeal, cruel and unusual punishments, Fourteenth Amendment and substantive due process became the fabric of a modern criminal trial. They were no longer abstract theories or rights.

A primary question raised by the above events, assuming the jury verdict was correct, is how could Roberts commit such heinous acts? His childhood seemed normal. He had loving and caring parents. There was no neglect or abuse. He was educated and above average in intelligence. Is there sometimes a defect in a person's genome which alone results in compulsive criminal behavior without regard to the harm to others? We are told that we were created by a loving God for a purpose. Why was David James Roberts created? Why were William, Elizabeth and Jenny Harold murdered?

If you have not already done so, there are two classic books that you should read which are examples of murder without conscience: *The Bad Seed* by William March, an excellent fictional story of Rhoda Penmark, age eight, and the "nonfiction novel" *In Cold Blood* by Truman Capote, a beautifully written true account of Dick Hickock and Perry Smith.

Finally, my sincere wish is that the telling of the Harold tragedy will contribute to a better understanding of our judicial process and of the Constitution, and, most of all, thereby give some meaning to the tragic deaths of William, Elizabeth and Jenny Harold.

John R. Berger
Angola, Indiana
January 1, 2016

JOHN R BERGER
January 1, 2016

BIBLIOGRAPHY

Marbury v. Madison, 1 Cranch 137 (1803)

Dred Scott v. Sandford, 19 How 393 (1857)

Buck v. Bell, 274 U.S. 200 (1927)

Mapp v. Ohio, 367 U.S. 643 (1961)

Gideon v. Wainwright, 372 U.S. 335 (1963)

Miranda v. Arizona, 384 U.S. 436 (1966)

Furman v. Georgia, 408 U.S. 238 (1972)

Woodson v. North Carolina, 428 U.S. 280 (1976)

French v. State of Indiana, 362 N.E. 2d 834 (1977)

Stump v. Sparkman, 435 U.S. 349 (1978)

Roberts v. State of Indiana, 375 N. E. 2d 215 (1978)

UNITED STATES CONSTITUTION

AMENDMENT IV (1791)

The right of the people to be secure in their persons, houses, papers, and effects, against unreasonable searches and seizures, shall not be violated, and no warrants shall issue, but upon probable cause, supported by Oath or affirmation and particularly describing the place to be searched, and the persons or things to be seized.

AMENDMENT V (1791)

No person shall be held to answer for a capital, or otherwise infamous crime, unless on a presentment or indictment of a Grand Jury, except in the cases in the land or naval forces, or in the Militia, when in actual service in time of War or public danger; nor shall any person be subject for the same offense to be twice put in jeopardy of life or limb; nor shall be compelled in any criminal case to be a witness against himself; nor be deprived of life, liberty, or property, without due process of law; nor shall private property be taken for public use, without just compensation.

AMENDMENT VI (1791)

In all criminal prosecutions, the accused shall enjoy the right to a speedy and public trial, by an impartial jury of the state and district wherein the crime shall have been committed, which district shall have been previously ascertained by law, and to be informed of the nature and cause of the accusation; to be confronted with the witnesses against him; to have compulsory process for obtaining witnesses in his favor; and to have the Assistance of Counsel for his defense.

AMENDMENT VIII (1791)

Excessive bail shall not be required, nor excessive fines imposed, nor cruel and unusual punishments inflicted.

AMENDMENT XI (1798)

The Judicial power of the United States shall not be construed to extend to any suit in law or equity, commenced or prosecuted against one of the United States by Citizens of another State, or by Citizens or Subjects of any Foreign State.

AMENDMENT XIII (1865)

Neither slavery nor involuntary servitude, except as a punishment for crime whereof the party shall have been duly convicted, shall exist within the United States, or any place subject to their jurisdiction.

The Congress shall have the power to enforce this article by appropriate legislation.
Note: Mississippi did not ratify until 2013.

AMENDMENT XIV (1868)

Section 1. All persons born or naturalized in the United States, and subject to the jurisdiction thereto, are citizens of the United States, and the State wherein they reside. No State shall make or enforce any law which shall abridge the privileges or immunities of citizens of the United States; nor shall any State deprive any person of life, liberty, or property, without due process of law; nor deny to any person within its jurisdiction the equal protection of the laws.

AMENDMENT XV (1870)

The right of the citizens of the United States to vote shall not be denied or abridged by the United States or by any State on account of race, color, or previous condition of servitude.

The Congress shall have the power to enforce this article by appropriate legislation.
Note: Tennessee did not ratify until 1997.

INDEPENDENCE HALL
PHILADELPHIA-1787

NOTES

1. The naming of Indiana and the XI Amendment: The area compromising the present state of Indiana was part of the Northwest Territory created by Congress in 1787. It was called Indiana Territory and was the area left after the Ohio Territory (1800), Michigan Territory (1805) and Illinois Territory (1809) were carved out. Indiana became a state in 1816 and included all of the area left of the original Indiana Territory. The name Indiana was borrowed by Congress and came from the name of about two million acres of land called Indiana (land of the Indians) in western Virginia Colony claimed by the Indiana Company by virtue of a 1768 deed from the Six Nations of the Iroquois. The name of this area was abandoned and available to Congress after 1798 when Virginia successfully asserted ownership of this area as Augusta County and the Indiana Company went out of existence. The Indiana Company had filed suit (a Bill in Equity) in the United States Supreme Court in 1792 against Virginia requesting the Supreme Court to issue an order to Virginia to cease interfering with the Indiana Company title. Virginia ignored all subpoenas issued by Chief Justice John Jay to appear before the Supreme Court. The subpoenas were titled, "The President of the United States to Henry Lee, Esquire, Governor of the Commonwealth of Virginia." Virginia successfully delayed the case until passage in 1798 of the XI Amendment which forbad such suits against a state. By virtue of this amendment, the suit was dismissed by the Supreme Court in 1798.

See *The Naming of Indiana* at www.in.gov/history/2805.htm for the complete story.

2. Angola had the dubious distinction of being the "Midwest Marriage Capitol" until about 1960. Indiana at that time did not require any residency or waiting period in order to be married. All adjoining states had strict waiting period requirements and Angola, being five miles from Michigan and Ohio, was a natural for couples who could not wait to be married (for a variety of reasons).

The marriage procedure took about two hours and was outlined in a handy flyer available at the Circuit Court Clerk's Office. First a couple was advised to go to one of the two friendly competing hospital labs (Elmhurst Hospital and Cameron Hospital) and have their blood tests taken for syphilis as required by Indiana law. If either tested positive, the couple was out of luck.

Other venereal diseases were inexplicably not tested. The next step was to wait for one hour, preferably at Ollie Bassett's restaurant (upstairs dining room and counter or newly remodeled basement bar) until the lab tests were reported to the clerk. Katherine Hepburn and her dog had eaten lunch at Bassett's in 1941. There was a photo of her with her dog at Bassett's.

CELEBRITY GETAWAY — Just after the turn of the century, Steuben County and Angola quickly became known as the hideout for the rich and famous. Gangsters, musicians and movie stars called Steuben's lakes their home away from home for decades, right up until the 1960s. Many of them, like Kathryn Hepburn (shown in this 1941 picture), had special booths reserved just for them at Bassett's Restaurant in Angola, on the southwest corner of Public Square.

After the hour, the couple would go to the clerk's office and apply for the marriage license.

On a usual Saturday, there would be a line of happy couples and friends stretching from the clerk's office, out the courthouse door, around the corner First National Bank and to the Post Office one block away. Many of the brides-to-be waiting in line, some obviously pregnant, wore complete long wedding gowns with veils. Many men wore tuxedos. Once the couple had completed the marriage application questionnaire for the clerk (Are either of you now married? Do either of you have any children? Are either of you insane?) the clerk would offer the couple a choice between the standard Indiana marriage license poorly printed on cheap thin paper or the deluxe version with faux leather cover and a genuine facsimile gold Indiana Seal for only twenty-five dollars more. The clerk was allowed to pocket the twenty-five dollars. Naturally the husband-to-be would choose the deluxe version to impress his beloved. Naturally, the clerk's position was highly contested at election time.

The next step was to find a justice of the peace or minister to marry the happy couple. All were conveniently located within a block of the court house. There were two justices of the peace, Con Smith and Harvey Shoup. Both had their wives available as official witnesses to the marriage ceremony. Both were adept at performing a meaningful but hasty ceremony with many quotations from the bible and other learned sources. After the ceremony, the justice signed the marriage certificate and bid farewell to the newlyweds. Both justices were amenable to accepting gratuities (the flyer suggested fifty dollars). The justice of the peace elections were also highly contested. If the couple wished to have the marriage performed by a minister, a small garden wedding chapel with flowers and an organist was available only one and a half blocks from the courthouse according to the map drawn on the flyer (suggested price including all services and gratuity-$100.00).

The nearby motels were filled with newlyweds. I think about half of the citizens of northern Ohio and southern Michigan had been married in Angola.

There were no mixed race couples waiting in line to be married. Indiana law from 1840 until 1965 made miscegenation a crime and provided that sexual intercourse or marriage between whites and blacks could be punished by a fine not to exceed $5,000.00 and imprisonment not to exceed twenty years. Blacks were defined as having one-eight or more Negro blood.

In addition to the Clerk of Court and Justice of the Peace positions, there was one other position which was highly sought after. This was Sheriff of Steuben County during the Prohibition era (1919-1933). One of the main routes for the transportation of liquor was from Canada to Detroit, then south to Ohio near Edon, then westward along what is now U.S. 20 through Steuben County and Angola, and then continuing westward to Chicago and Al Capone and associates. It was reported that bootleggers were often met in Steuben County at the Indiana-Ohio line by the Steuben County Sheriff who was collecting donations to the police benevolent society. It was an early version of the Indiana Toll Road.

According to a 1930 article in the Steuben Republican, the local newspaper:

"By virtue of the Prohibition law (the 1919 Volstead Act) Steuben County has recently suffered several black eyes. The federal government charged that Steuben County Sheriff Charles Zimmerman aided bootleggers in transporting liquor through the county. Charles Zimmerman faced three separate criminal law suits in federal court in Fort Wayne, two for violating the Prohibition law and one for murder of a witness. Zimmerman was also said to have been paid protection money by a Steuben County resident who sold and manufactured liquor in Steuben County.

In one example dated 1927, Zimmerman allegedly transported twenty cases of whisky from the Powers School, which is just west of the Ohio line, to Angola. To keep his illegal activity flowing, Zimmerman allegedly paid protection money to a federal prohibition officer through an Angola attorney. Zimmerman obtained dubious acquittals on all three charges. In one case a witness changed his story and refused to finger the sheriff. In another case, the government's witness, the officer to whom Zimmerman allegedly paid bribes, disappeared just prior to trial."

Zimmerman was vigorously defended by a powerful and expensive defense team. Among the attorneys representing Zimmerman were Angola attorneys Alphonso C. Wood, soon to become an Indiana Appellate Judge (1931-1938), his son, Theodore Wood, later to become President of Tri-State University, and Dudley Gleason, Sr. of the firm of Gleason & Gleason.

3.   I was only threatened twice. The first time was during the Roberts' case. The second was after I had left the bench. Having courthouse security would not have saved me from either threat. In the later threat, I received a call from a Michigan probation officer after he had completed an "exit interview." He had just had a conversation with a convict named Clark who was about to be released after five years in a Michigan prison for arson. I had sentenced Clark to jail in Indiana for arson about ten years before for burning down a cottage at Hamilton Lake. The officer had asked the convict what he intended to do after release, expecting an answer concerning where he would live and work. Clark replied, "Well, the first thing I am going to do is go back to Angola and burn Judge Berger's house down and I hope he is in it." I thanked the officer for this information and wondered what I could do about it. The next day I received information from our local police that Clark had indeed burned a house down early that morning but that the house was in Ashley, a town about fifteen miles away.

I guess I was lucky and someone else was higher on Clark's "To Do" list.

4.   Cincinnati was known as the "Queen City of the West" by virtue of being the early commercial metropolis of the Ohio Valley. I grew up in Cincinnati but the main attraction to me as a seventeen year old was across the Ohio River in the city of Newport, Kentucky, and the Tropicana nightclub. During the Civil War and for the next hundred years Newport in Campbell

199

County was known as "The Sin City of the South" with rampant prostitution, gambling and national-crime-syndicate operations. The story of Newport, and of the Notre Dame, New York Yanks and Cleveland Browns quarterback hero, George Ratterman, who ran as the reform candidate for sheriff of Campbell County in 1961, is dramatically set forth in *The Great Kentucky Scandal*, an October 24, 1961 article by Bill Davidson in Look Magazine. The story starts with police entering a motel room at the Glenn Hotel (connected to the Tropicana) and finding Ratterman allegedly clad only with a shirt and socks in bed with a long-legged strip-teaser named "April Flowers" dressed in a slave robe with leopard-skin design with her bosom showing. The state court trial of Ratterman for soliciting prostitution came to a sudden end when the prosecutor dismissed the charges after hearing evidence that Ratterman may have been drugged. The story ends just before a newly appointed United States Attorney General Bobby Kennedy sends a young federal prosecuting attorney, Ronald Goldfarb, from Washington to Newport to try and obtain federal indictments against the participants in Ratterman's false arrest and an attorney, Charles E. Lester, who is mentioned in the Look article and had represented some of the defendants in prior state charges arising out of the events of that fateful night. See www.nkyviews.com/campbell/text/txt_newport_look.htm for the full article.

1961 SHERIFF CANDIDATE   1950 NEW YORK YANKS
GEORGE RATTERMAN

My research indicates the following later events.

At the insistence of thirty-four year old newly appointed U.S. Attorney General Robert Kennedy, the brother of President Jack Kennedy, a federal indictment was obtained and filed in federal court in October of 1961against Charles E. Lester, a well known and respected criminal

200

defense attorney; Edward "Marty" Buccieri, the owner of the Tropicana and Glenn Hotel; Tito Carinci, the manager of the Tropicana; and three police officers, Quitter, White and Ciafardini. Robert Kennedy would preside over a Justice Department with over thirty thousand people. He had limited legal experience and had never been in a courtroom.

The charges were misdemeanor conspiracy to violate the civil rights of George Ratterman. They were charged with having "a common agreement to discredit Ratterman by falsely arresting and charging him." The government was represented by lead attorney twenty-nine year old Ronald Goldfarb, two assisting attorneys and a special FBI consultant, Frank Staab, who was convinced that Lester was behind much of the legal arrangements shielding illegal operations in Newport. Staab had made an exhaustive investigation throughout the United States and had held over five hundred interviews in an attempt to uncover evidence against these defendants and others. Robert Kennedy wanted to charge the defendants with kidnapping across state lines but was unsuccessful in obtaining any evidence thereof. Goldfarb and his legal assistants were assigned to the case by Robert Kennedy. They were special prosecutors in the Justice Department's Organized Crime and Racketeering Section. They were sent from Washington to prosecute these misdemeanor charges. Goldfarb was all excited. This was his big chance to make a name for himself prosecuting "mobsters."

A federal jury trial was held and the jury could not agree on a verdict. Even though a retrial of a misdemeanor charge is rare and very expensive, the federal prosecutor, Ronald Goldfarb, with extreme pressure from Robert Kennedy, presented the case again to a new jury. In August of 1963, the second jury convicted Lester and Buccieri of conspiring with the police to have the police arrest an innocent Ratterman. The jury decided however that Carinci was not guilty of conspiracy and that the police, Quitter, White and Ciafardini, did not knowingly falsely arrest and charge Ratterman and were found not guilty! The only evidence against Lester, as set forth in the above Look article, was that he had asked photographer Thomas Withrow to contact Buccieri about taking some photographs. Whose photographs, where and when was not discussed by Lester. The photographs were never taken. Lester explained in his testimony that it was his understanding that Withrow would be hired to take photographs of patrons at the Tropicana nightclub, not of Ratterman in the Glenn Hotel room.

Lester and Buccieri were sentenced by federal district court Judge Swinford to twelve months in federal prison, the maximum allowed by law. Such a severe penalty was almost unheard of. Lester was 61 years old and had no prior felony charges.

The defendants Buccieri and Lester appealed to the federal Sixth Circuit Court of Appeals. The defendants argued, "If police officers were not guilty and did not conspire with defendants, how could defendants conspire with the police officers?" The prosecution realized that there was a serious potential of reversible error and hoped that in the appellate judges' deliberation there might be a subconscious undertow toward upholding convictions to assure that everyone involved would not go free. They hoped the appellate judges, who did not agree with the jury's not guilty decisions as to the police officers, would unwittingly nullify the pure law to arrive at a "just" decision upholding the guilty verdict for Buccieri and Lester.

The "subconscious undertow" perhaps won out. The appellate court sustained the conviction by a split decision-two to one. The majority stated that Lester and Buccieri could be found guilty of conspiring with innocent police officers to commit a crime which was never committed! The United States Supreme Court declined to review the case.

Buccieri was granted an early release on parole but Lester was not granted early release. He was first held in a minimum security federal prison in Alabama. When Robert Kennedy heard of this he prevailed upon the justice department to have Lester transferred to a maximum security federal prison in southern Illinois which primarily held rapists and murderers. While there, Lester lost over forty pounds. Upon his release he slowly recovered his physical health but until his death still carried psychological scars.

At the instigation of Robert Kennedy, the Internal Revenue Service with the assistance of the FBI extensively pursued Lester in an attempt to prove income tax evasion. They were unsuccessful.

In spite of all the time, money and energy spent by Robert Kennedy's Justice Department to clean out the "organized crime and mobsters" in Campbell County, these two misdemeanor convictions were the only ones obtained. Kennedy's frustration was taken out on attorney Lester and Buccieri. The true mobsters just moved on.

Ronald Goldfarb is a well known and respected Washington, D.C. attorney, speaker, author and literary agent.

Juanita Hodges a/k/a "April Flowers" continued her dancing first in Louisville, then in Alabama, and later in Port Huron, Michigan.

George Ratterman served four years as sheriff. After that he was a color commentator for radio and television. On occasion he was a financial advisor. He never practiced law. He died in November of 2007 at the age of eighty of complications from Alzheimer's disease.

Bruce Lester, the son of Charles Lester, became a respected judge of the Kentucky Appellate Court for over twenty years and retired recently as Chief Judge.

Two years after the Lester decision, Robert Kennedy was assassinated on June 6, 1968.

Charles E. Lester was my mother's brother, my favorite Uncle Charlie.

5. The Korean War was the "forgotten war" and most civilians went about their lives oblivious to the fact that thousands of American young men were giving their lives for our country. It was not even called a "war." It was called a "conflict." I had a good friend in college who had remained in the Army reserve after active service in WW II. He was just completing his senior year at college when he received notice in May, 1950, to report for active duty in three days. He was killed six months later in North Korea just south of the Yalu River by soldiers of the invading Fifteenth Chinese Field Army. He was twenty-four. He was one of the thirty-three thousand six hundred and eighty-six soldiers who gave their lives "to stop the spread of communism."

6. In May of my last year at Harvard Law I applied for a direct commission as First Lieutenant in the newly established contract procurement department of the Air Force located at Wright Patterson Air Force Base in Ohio. Two other classmates and I were asked to come to the Pentagon for interviews with the Secretary of the Air Force. We arrived by air the evening before and I will always remember circling over Washington and seeing the lights of the beautiful buildings and monuments of Washington.

The Pentagon and Secretary's chambers were very impressive-especially to a small town boy. During the interview the Secretary asked us what our class standings were. The first to respond was a classmate who was the president of the Harvard Law Review (like President Barack Obama) who stated that he was first in our class. Next my other classmate stated that he was third in our class. The Secretary turned to me and asked, "Mr. Berger, what was your standing?" With some trepidation I answered that I was one thirty-sixth! I felt somewhat embarrassed.

We all were accepted into the program (I was swept in on my classmates' coattails). I was excited and looked forward to three years serving my country during the Korean War in Ohio.

I received a brief note from the Air Force in July that the program had been abandoned (together with my commission).

Determined to be an officer, I then applied to the United States Coast Guard. I had always enjoyed boats and the water. They sent me to Cleveland for a physical and four hour written examination. I was accepted and ordered to appear on December 1, 1953, at the Coast Guard Academy in New London, Connecticut to be sworn in as an Ensign to begin my training. There was one condition-I had to be released from my draft board in Cincinnati (Laura Wingerberg, Clerk). I am glad that I did not waste money on purchasing several Coast Guard uniforms.

7. The requirements to practice law in Indiana have an interesting history. Most lawyers after the Revolution had a difficult time being allowed to practice law. The people rejected them as being instruments of and supporters of the English common law, and of not being loyal supporters of the Revolution. Most had been Tories. All things thought to be English were rejected. As a result, most states passed laws denying the right to practice law unless loyalty was proven. New York State passed a typical law which required a jury to find that an applicant to practice law had been "a good and zealous friend to the American cause" before being licensed.

By 1850 the prejudice against lawyers had diminished. However, the Jacksonian theory of the egalitarian rights of the common man was becoming preeminent and it was thought that every man had a natural right to practice any lawful calling he chose. As a result of this philosophy, most states passed statutes or had constitutional provisions that did not require a license or any other particular requirements or qualifications to practice law except being of good moral character. One early Indiana statute added an additional requirement-the applicant had to take an oath that he had not participated in any part of a dual since January 1, 1819. The Indiana Constitution of 1851 in Article VII, Sec. 21, stated, "Every person of good moral character, being a voter, shall be entitled to admission to practice law in all courts of justice." Therefore, basically the only requirements to practice law were to be a voter of "good moral character", which, as one whit put it, was the one qualification most practitioners plainly lacked. However, egalitarianism only went so far in 1851. The same 1851 Constitution denied women and Negroes the right to vote. Since women could not vote until 1921 and Negroes not until 1881, were they entitled to practice law before then?

As early as 1893, a courageous white lady named Antoinette Dakin Leach applied to the Greene Circuit Court for admission to the bar. The circuit court judge found that she was a citizen of Indiana, over the age of twenty-one, of good moral character, and possessed sufficient knowledge of the law to qualify her to practice. However, the circuit judge denied admission as she was not a voter as the Indiana Constitution required. On appeal, the Indiana Supreme Court determined that the Constitution did indeed secure the right of a voter to be admitted to practice, but it did not affirmatively state that others (non voters) could not also have this right. Therefore, the Court ruled Antoinette should be admitted to the practice of law.

I wonder if the justices in arriving at their decision had received advice from their wives similar to that given by Abigail Adams to her husband John in 1776 when he was on his way to the Constitutional Convention to "remember the ladies and be more generous and favorable to them than your ancestors" when fashioning laws for the new nation.

Sixty-three years later when I first started to practice law in 1956, there was only one woman attorney admitted to practice law in northeast Indiana. Now about half of law school students are women.

Pursuant to this 1851 Constitutional provision, attorneys were usually admitted to the bar by the local Circuit Court judge. There was no requirement of any law school, other formal education, law studies or experience. Many obtained their legal training by "reading law" in the law office of an established attorney. They were basically self taught. It was not until 1932 that the Indiana Constitution was amended to repeal the provision that any voter of good moral character could practice law.

After 1932, Indiana by statute or Supreme Court Rule gradually set forth requirements to practice law. Ultimately, graduation from an accredited law school and successful completion of the bar examination would be required. These laws and rules allowed all those persons who were currently admitted to the bar to continue to practice under "grandfather clauses." They became known as "Constitutional lawyers." For a very interesting discussion of these issues and many more see The History of Indiana Law, 2006, Ohio University Press.

8. On a dark and wet December 14, 1953, morning at 5 a.m., I boarded a bus in Angola with ten other draftees, all from local farm families, destination Indianapolis. Upon arrival we, together with forty other draftees, were told to strip and get in line to be examined by a doctor. The doctors determined that we were all physically fit even though I kept reminding the doctors that I had rheumatic fever as a child.

We then were told to stand in a straight line facing an Army Lieutenant and to raise our right hands. We did so and took our oath to protect and defend. We were told to take one step forward and by doing so became a part of the United States Army.

I was issued my official identification "dog tags" which had impressed thereon "John R. Berger US 55448329 Blood: A Religion: C." The "US" in my serial number differentiated me from those who had voluntarily enlisted. The enlistees were "RA" and considered to be a different breed.

It is hard to describe my emotions upon taking the oath and being a member of the Army. I do remember being very proud to serve my country and to begin such service as a private equally with my fellow draftees from all walks of life. I was always very proud to wear my Army uniform even though during the Korean Conflict some civilians looked down upon me as a serviceman.

9. On my arrival at Fort Leonard Wood at 1 a.m. dressed in a gray tweed suit and striped tie, I was told to report immediately to the mess hall for KP duty. My first military duties consisted of mopping the floors and washing dishes, pots and pans until 3 p.m. I then reported to my assigned barracks and was issued bedding, a trunk to be placed at the foot of my bunk, an M1 rifle, and basic toiletries which included a blade razor (I had only used an electric shaver before).

My only experience with a rifle was as an eight year old. I had a Red Ryder BB gun and shot a starling. The bird tumbled to the ground and flopped around. Apparently I had broken his wing. Immediately I felt terrible and tried to nurse him back to good health. With my gentle care he lasted three days. I buried him with a headstone marked "Sam". This was the last and only time that I shot a rifle without cause.

Exhausted and dirty, in my gray tweed suit, my service to my country began. I was issued a uniform three days later.

In the fourth week of basic training I was called in from the machine gun range for an interview pursuant to my previous application to the Army Judge Advocate's Office (the law branch of the Army). In my dirty uniform and with four hours sleep I was grilled on the intricacies of law by a panel of one Captain and two First Lieutenants. I distinctly remember one question. I was asked to explain in detail the "hearsay rule" and as many of the exceptions thereto as I could recall (there are about thirty). This is probably one of the most difficult legal principals. The "hearsay rule" is an evidentiary trial rule on the admissibility of certain testimony. The rule can be simply stated as, "A witness can not testify as to what he heard another person say in order to prove the truth of the facts stated by such person." Somehow I stumbled through the interview.

I did not hear anything concerning my application until about twenty-two months later when I was called in before my commanding officer. He explained to me that I had passed the examination and had been recommended for acceptance into the Judge Advocate's Office. However, the examining board had been improperly constituted. The board should have had two Captains instead of the one at the board examination. Therefore I would have to be examined again. He assured me that I would undoubtedly pass the next examination and be appointed a First Lieutenant. I would have to serve three more years of active duty in the Army. Since I was due to be discharged in two months, I respectfully withdrew my application.

10. I remember clearly my first civil and criminal cases. Both were before the Steuben Circuit Court judge, the Honorable Harris Hubbard. Both cases made clear to me the difficulties I would have trying to establish a law practice in the Steuben County legal environment.

In my first civil case I represented a foreign (Chicago) supplier of minnows who had sold the minnows to a local (a Steuben County voter) bait store. The bait store refused to pay for the

207

minnows claiming that the minnows had died of some mysterious disease about one week after delivery. I obtained an expert in minnow diseases who testified that the minnows were not diseased when delivered but were contaminated by the condition of the bait store minnow tanks. There was no other evidence as to the cause of the disease. At the conclusion of the evidence, Judge Hubbard announced his decision (the case was heard by the court rather than by a jury). He stated that the evidence clearly showed that the minnows were in perfect condition when they were delivered. I was in seventh heaven. I was about to win my first case and could represent to prospective clients that I had never lost a case. The judge then said, "However." I knew that these words were the death knell. The judge then stated that since the delivery of the minnows had been on a Sunday, the sales contract was void and the bait store therefore did not have to pay for the minnows. The judge's decision was erroneous, of course, as Indiana law has never declared Sunday contracts void. To appeal the decision to the Indiana Appellate Court would have cost about twenty times the value of the minnows! Case closed. The attorney for the bait store, the judge's brother Kenny Hubbard, had won another one.

In my first criminal case, I was appointed as pauper counsel for the defendant by Judge Hubbard. There were about eight other eligible attorneys but Judge Hubbard obviously thought that this case was just right for me as a young attorney trying to establish a law practice. As a new attorney I could hardly refuse such an appointment. The defendant, a recent resident of Mt. Clemens Michigan, who was just passing through Angola, was accused of kidnapping the daughter of a prominent Angola businessman on her way home from grade school. Thankfully, she was found alive a day later about fifty miles away. She identified the defendant as the person who had kidnapped her. By representing such a person this certainly was an excellent chance for me to become well thought of and accepted by the Angola community.

Having taken my oath as an attorney to faithfully represent a client, and being young and naïve, I earnestly began my representation. I immediately requested a change of judge which by law had to be granted. This further endeared me to Judge Hubbard.

My client stated that he had an iron clad alibi. He told me that at the time of the abduction he was living in Mt. Clemens and had in fact at that time been at the St. Francis Cemetery in Mt. Clemens placing flowers on the grave of his mother. He remembered that when visiting his mother's grave that twin two day old boys were being interred.

I took off for Mt. Clemens, about 100 miles to the northeast and just north of Detroit, in my parents' 1952 Buick Road Master station wagon. The trip was uneventful except for the fact that since the Buick weighed about a ton and the brakes were woefully underpowered, it was very difficult to bring the car to a stop. Somehow I made it.

My first stop was at the address the defendant gave me for the place where he stayed. The defendant was sure some other resident would remember him being there on the day of the abduction. It was difficult to find the address. It was in what appeared to be a slum area. I was somewhat hesitant to enter the building at the address.

My sociology professor at Hillsdale College had written a book (required purchase) about his experiences at the Bowery in Brooklyn which he entitled Flophouse. I was now truly entering a flophouse. The building was three stories. There was a small office on the first floor. The rest of the building contained single rooms. There was filth and refuse everywhere. I found only three persons. One was sitting in a stairwell and obviously drunk. He was unable to communicate with me. I saw another person on the third floor through an open door lying naked on a stained mattress, apparently asleep or passed out. I did not disturb him. The third was the "manager" who was preparing some soup in a makeshift kitchen. He had no recollection of the defendant. He did give me the direction to St. Francis Cemetery.

I was able to find the cemetery and the Rectory of the adjoining church. I located the Sextant and he was able to examine the Record of Burials. He said that he remembered the twin boys' burials. He examined the records and they showed that the burials had been one day before the abduction in Angola. That was the end of the alibi!

Upon return to Angola I met with the prosecuting attorney to see if a plea bargain could be agreed upon. Both of us wanted to avoid a trial in which the little girl would have to testify. I told the defendant that I was trying to negotiate a plea bargain. The next day the defendant sent a demand from the jail to the judge written on a paper hand towel that the judge remove me from representing him. The defendant stated that, "I had spilled my guts to the prosecutor." The judge, to my great relief, replaced me as the attorney for the defendant. The defendant subsequently did enter a plea of guilty pursuant to a plea agreement.

11. There is a sad sidebar to my defeat of Judge Sisler which connected causally to three murders. If Judge Sisler had been elected, none of the following would have happened.

209

After his loss of the judgeship, with the assistance of his father in law, Judge Sisler obtained a job in Washington, D.C., as a lobbyist for the National Rifle Association. About a year after arriving in Washington, he was confronted at his front door one evening by an armed angry black man who stated that his sister had been raped by a middle aged white man and that the man reportedly lived in Sisler's house. An argument ensued and Judge Sisler was fatally shot.

A police investigation followed, the man was arrested and subsequently found guilty of Voluntary Manslaughter.

The chief investigating officer was Bobby Moore. Later Bobby Moore and Barbara Sisler, Judge Sisler's widow, were married and took up residence in the Town of Fremont in the northeast corner of Steuben County. Bobby became the Town Marshall.

About a year later, while Barbara Sisler Moore was on the phone talking with her daughter, Barbara stated that she had to leave the phone for a minute because her husband Bobby needed to talk to her. Her daughter overheard an apparent argument between Barbara and Bobby and then gunshots.

When the police arrived at the Moore home they found Barbara dead. Bobby stated to police that there had been an argument, that Barbara had threatened to kill him with a gun, and that he fired at her in self defense. Bobby Moore was never charged with the death of his wife.

About a month after the death of Barbara Moore, on a warm July 1988 evening just before sun down, Bobby Moore was shot in the head by a high powered rifle discharged from some distance away. He died minutes later. Barbara's son, Sam Sisler, reportedly was an initial suspect but no evidence was ever found to connect him to the murder. No charges were ever filed.

12. The matters presented to a Circuit Court judge are varied and challenging.

The matters presenting the most difficult choices to me were child custody in divorce cases, disposition of juvenile matters, and sentencing in criminal cases. All divorce and juvenile matters are presented to a judge for decision. A jury is not allowed.

In Indiana a person can obtain a divorce if there are "irreconcilable differences." This is quite different from the traditional divorce requirements of proof of adultery or incurable insanity. These strict rules gave rise to the hiring of private investigators who would attempt to take a photograph of the erring partner "in flagrante delicto." Also, what is "incurable insanity" and

210

how do you prove it? Therefore now in Indiana, a person can always obtain a divorce by testifying, "My wife and I disagree on almost everything and there is no chance that we can get back together again." Note: Indiana now allows by agreement no-fault divorce and the waiver of a trial. Unlike most other states, Indiana does not provide for alimony (support payments) to a husband or wife unless he or she is severely mentally or physically disabled. This does not provide much protection to the wife who drops out of school, gets a job to help her husband through medical school, has three children while her husband is building his practice, and is then divorced by her husband "for irreconcilable differences." She is left to rear the children while her husband marries his nurse and lives happily ever after. She will have to support herself with only a high school education!

The Indiana divorce statute was amended when I was judge. The Indiana legislature in their infinite wisdom thought that it was deleterious to use the term "divorce" and amended the law to provide that thereafter the term would be "dissolution of marriage." Therefore after the amendment it was improper for a wife to say to her husband, "If you hit me one more time I'm gunna stick your ass in jail, take the kids and divorce you." The proper comment would be, "Honey, if you cannot conform your actions to accepted standards, I might have to seek incarceration for you and file a Petition for Dissolution of Marriage."

Presiding over divorce cases was an eye opener for me. I guess I had led a sheltered life. I had parents that loved each other who never raised their voices in anger and a wife who was all things wondrous. It was difficult for me to listen to testimony from people who had been in love and had promised "to love and honor until death do us part" tear each other apart in the hope of obtaining a larger property settlement. Usually custody was an afterthought. The mother traditionally obtained custody of young children.

Occasionally both the husband and wife would seek a divorce. Each party wanted bragging rights. "The Judge gave me the divorce because of the way my husband (wife) treated me."

In one divorce case which stands out in my memory, a childless couple in their 60s both wanted a divorce but they could not agree on who would get the Cadillac and some wedding presents they had received five years before. The husband was represented by Dudley Gleason, Jr. of the firm of Gleason & Gleason (father and son), a sixty two year old constitutional lawyer who seemed to always quote the bible when making any statement to a judge or jury. He was

211

about five feet tall, robust and had a deep resonant voice. It was almost like hearing God speak. The only issue at the trial was the division of their property. I was therefore somewhat surprised when Dudley offered into evidence on behalf of the husband, without objection of opposing counsel, seven photographs of the wife in a Holiday Inn motel room in Florida which were taken on a recent vacation. The photographs were taken by the husband and showed his wife completely nude in various poses. I asked Dudley the relevancy of the photographs and he stated, "Your Honor, any woman who would allow herself to be photographed naked is immoral, is condemned before the eyes of God, and should not be allowed to share in my client's worldly goods." I was preoccupied with the pictures which showed a rather plump old woman with large sagging breasts. I could not imagine anyone that old cavorting sexually around a hotel room. Remember, I was in my early 40s. I have since changed my mind.

A divorce case was never really over until the youngest child reached eighteen. The parties seemed to always be coming back to court to revise the amount of child support ("My husband got a new job and he is making more now" or "He is spending a ton of money on that fat girl friend of his and her children"); to change visitation ("I do not want my daughter around that whore he is living with"); custody ("I just can't handle Joshua anymore. He is out of control and smokes pot. It's his father's turn"); and to request that the husband be put in jail for non support or failure to abide by a visitation order ("He makes a ton of money but spends it all on booze, punch cards and girlfriends and has not paid support for four months" or "I have the kids ready for visitation every other Sunday at 2 p.m. but he rarely shows up to pick them up and even if he does, he returns them dirty and late every time").

Miracles do happen though. Often I had a father testify in a non support case that he really wanted to catch up on his back support (usually several thousand dollars) and help his six children, but even though he had a good job, he had no money available. About the second day of serving an indeterminate jail sentence for contempt of court, the husband would somehow come up with the money and pay the entire back support-a miracle!

Juvenile court was a heartbreaker. Anyone up to eighteen was considered a juvenile in Indiana and there was a distinct body of law for them which was different from adult criminal law. The emphasis in juvenile law was help rather than punishment. A juvenile could not be originally charged with a criminal law violation. A juvenile was charged with "An act of delinquency, to wit: taking cash at gun point from the cash register at the Martin Gas Station." The judge was to act as "parens patriae" or an enlightened father, understanding, fair, but firm. The judge was to exercise the conscience of the community. When I first started to practice law, a juvenile offender when caught was held in jail for a day or so and then brought before the judge. The prosecutor presented the facts and, after the juvenile made any statement he desired, the judge would immediately decide if the juvenile had committed the offense and if so, what should be done about it. Usually there were no witnesses other than a police officer. The juvenile was not represented by an attorney. His parents were allowed to be present and make a statement. When I became judge, the law had changed. The juvenile was always represented by an attorney (at county expense usually), the hearing was conducted like an adult criminal trial, and a final decision could not be made by the judge until the juvenile had been evaluated by the probation department or other experts deemed necessary.

Most juvenile offenders were male. I had a few delinquent girls but their offenses were minor such as shoplifting or skipping school. If the offense was serious, such as armed robbery, the minor could be "waived" by the judge to adult criminal court and the prosecutor was instructed by the judge to file adult criminal charges against the juvenile. All proceedings thereafter including sentencing to prison were treated as if the juvenile were an adult.

In juvenile matters I tried very hard to understand the cause of the delinquency and structure a proper response to help the juvenile. In some cases this might even entail a stay at the county jail. Many times the probation officer and I failed to help the juvenile. Sad to say, even at fourteen or fifteen, it was often too late.

In one juvenile case, I visited with the juvenile quietly in my chambers in an attempt to find the cause of his acts. He had broken into four cottages around Crooked Lake and stolen some electronics. He was seventeen, the son of a local professional and had supportive parents. I asked him why he had broken into the cottages and his sole explanation was, "Because it was easy." Go figure. I gave up delving into juvenile psychiatry.

In another juvenile case, I thought that I may have been successful in rehabilitation. Charlie was seventeen and had been involved in several burglaries about six months before. He had been reporting to the probation officer on a regular basis and on one of these visits to the probation officer, I talked with Charlie. I asked how he was doing and if there was anything I or the probation officer could do to help him. He stated that he was doing real well, had gone back to school and had a part time job. He wanted to thank us for helping him. I remember that evening, while relaxing with a glass of wine (white zinfandel), telling my wife Susanna about Charlie and how pleased we were about his apparent success. In the early morning hours of the next day, Charlie was arrested in Michigan after blowing the door of a safe at a Sears. Under Michigan law he was an adult at seventeen and he was later found guilty and sentenced to eight years in prison.

Most of my civil suits involved automobile accidents. If the plaintiff could prove that the defendant was negligent (that the defendant drove the vehicle below the standard of care that a reasonable man would have exercised which was the proximate cause of damages to plaintiff's vehicle or person), and that plaintiff was not negligent, the plaintiff was entitled to damages. Determining personal injury damages was difficult if pain and suffering were involved. Doctor and hospital bills and lost wages were usually easy to prove. But how much should a judge or jury award for the loss of an eye, both legs, brain damage, paralysis or pain? I have heard plaintiffs' attorneys state to the jury to aid them in determining damages for pain, "How much money would you take per day constantly to have severe headaches every day (or not be able to walk) for the rest of your life? Just multiply that amount by the life expectancy of the plaintiff."

I also presided over several civil cases against medical doctors for malpractice (medical negligence). Indiana had an interesting negligence evidentiary law which was only applicable to medical negligence. In order to prove medical negligence, the plaintiff must produce at least one licensed medical doctor as a witness who testifies that he or she is familiar with the accepted standard of medical care in the community and that the actions of the defendant doctor fell below this standard. Two cases were brought by the same attorney against the same doctor.

The first malpractice case involved a claim by a married couple for damages for the birth of their ninth child. The first eight children joined as plaintiffs. The defendant doctor had performed a sterilization tubal ligation upon the wife after her eighth child was born. This procedure, as were all previous deliveries, was paid for by the County Welfare Department. About ten months later, the wife gave birth to a normal boy. The wife claimed damages for her pain and suffering in childbirth and for support for the ninth child until he was eighteen. The husband claimed damages for his loss of consortium (sex) with his wife during the pregnancy and for support for the ninth child until he was eighteen. The other eight children claimed damages in that there would be less money for their care and less love and affection for them since they would now have to share with a ninth child. The plaintiffs wanted the defendant doctor to support the ninth child until he was eighteen!

The defendant denied all claims. He also claimed that there was no such negligence law in Indiana, and that the plaintiff wife should have had an abortion or placed the child for adoption if the child was not wanted. It was their duty to mitigate (lessen) damages. The plaintiffs stated that they wanted and loved the child.

This type of action has become to be known as a "wrongful birth" action as contrasted with the traditional "wrongful death" negligence action. Whether this type of negligence action should be allowed as common law in Indiana had not been presented to any Indiana court. It was a case of first impression and I was being asked to establish a "wrongful birth" negligence action as part of the common law of Indiana. After extensive research I determined that only two states had ruled on this. Michigan had allowed such an action and Delaware had not. The Delaware Supreme Court thought that the benefits of having a healthy child far exceeded any damages and therefore, as a matter of law, since plaintiffs had no damages there could not be any recovery. The Michigan Supreme Court thought that a jury should be given the opportunity to decide if in fact the plaintiffs were damaged. In the Michigan case the defendant was a pharmacist who had mistakenly given the plaintiff wife sleeping pills instead of the prescribed birth control pills.

I followed the Michigan rule and allowed the matter to proceed to trial. The plaintiffs had the required licensed doctor witness who testified not in person but by deposition. The doctor practiced general medicine in Wyoming but stated that he was well acquainted with the medical standards of Steuben County, Indiana, as to a proper tubal ligation since he was originally from Steuben County. He stated that in his opinion the defendant must have failed to properly perform the operation as a child was conceived. His deposition was read to the jury by the plaintiffs' attorney who had a deep voice and looked like a doctor. The jury did not know that in fact the doctor had a high voice and was not impressive at all.

The defendant had two imminently qualified tubal ligation specialists as witnesses. They had performed hundreds of such operations and testified that the procedure followed by the defendant was according to accepted medical practice. They further testified that even with a proper tubal ligation operation, sometimes nature would reconnect the cut tube and pregnancy could occur. The jury found that the defendant was not negligent. There was therefore no need for the jury to determine if there were any damages to plaintiffs.

The second malpractice case involved a couple in their late 50s. The plaintiffs were represented by the same attorney and the suit was against the same medical doctor. The doctor was alleged to have botched a vasectomy. The plaintiff husband claimed that after the operation he had developed two nodules on his penis and as a result he had experienced extreme pain when engaging in intercourse. This condition lasted for about three months and until the same doctor performed a minor procedure and removed the nodules. The husband could not claim damages for the expense of the operations as the County Welfare Department had paid for these. He did however claim damages for pain and suffering during intercourse for the three months. The wife joined as a plaintiff and claimed damages for diminished pleasure during intercourse because of the discomforting effect of the nodules. She further claimed that during intercourse her husband perspired a lot and would keep crying out, which indicated to her that her husband was in extreme pain. This considerably lessened her pleasure to her great damage. The plaintiff husband claimed ten thousand dollars as damages and the plaintiff wife claimed five thousand dollars as damages. The plaintiffs' attorney on direct examination of the wife in order to attempt to prove the extent of damages elicited the fact that they had intercourse at least once a day. Upon cross examination the doctor's attorney asked the wife, "Surely you did not have relations every day for ninety days?" She replied modestly, "Oh yes, we were so in love." The jurors during all of the testimony about fell out of their chairs leaning forward to not miss a word of the testimony. I had a hard time keeping a judicial demeanor and thought to myself "fantastic." The jury returned a verdict awarding damages of ten thousand dollars to the husband and five thousand dollars to the wife. If my calculations are correct, and assuming the number of assignations alleged are correct, this would amount to about $166.67 per pop (less 33% attorney fees).

My thoughts of "fantastic" during the testimony of the wife came from one of my favorite jokes. It seems that two married ladies were discussing their past summer vacations. The first lady stated that her handsome, wonderful and generous husband had first taken her to Paris and bought her all of the latest French perfumes. The other lady replied "fantastic." The first lady

216

then stated that her husband had then taken her to Moscow and bought her a gorgeous full length Russian sable coat. The other lady again replied "fantastic." The first lady then stated that her husband had then taken her to Rome and bought her many beautiful Italian leather shoes and handbags. The other lady again replied "fantastic." The first lady then inquired of the second lady "And what did you do this summer?" The second lady answered that her husband had paid tuition for her to take a two week charm school course for ladies. "And what did you learn?" the first lady inquired. The second lady responded "I learned to say fantastic instead of bullshit."

I presided over many criminal cases. One thing I surmised was that there must have been a special class at the police academy which would assist an officer in testifying concerning why he or she had searched a vehicle or arrested a driver for driving under the influence. When the prosecutor would ask a police witness at trial why the vehicle was searched or the defendant arrested, the reply was always, "I observed what appeared to be a green leafy plant like material (marihuana) protruding from under the front seat." or "I observed what appeared to be the butt of a gun protruding from under the front seat." or "The driver had blurry eyes, slurred speech, and there was a strong odor of alcohol." The exact words were used in every trial!

During my tenure as judge there were not many drug charges filed. They were mostly possession of a small amount of marihuana. Meth was unknown then. Not as now where almost every other old farm house (and quite a few automobiles) in northeast Indiana have active and profitable meth labs. It seems that about every week a farm house or car is blowing or burning up due to faulty recipes.

Two drug cases involved more serious offenses. Both incidentally involved dogs. The first case was commenced by a request by the prosecutor that I issue a search warrant. The Fourth Amendment provides that no search warrant shall be issued unless there is presented to a judge an affidavit of probable cause to believe that the search will lead to the discovery of certain described evidence. The affidavit must be made by a person who is reputable who has direct knowledge of the facts. In this case the reputable person was a dog!

The dog had been on regular patrol for the Postal Department at the San Diego, California, port and when sniffing a certain large package being mailed from Thailand to a person with an address of Jimmerson Lake, Angola, Indiana, indicated that the package had hashish (a high grade marihuana) inside. Usually a package would have had an outer layer of coffee beans to

217

disguise the distinct odor. The Thai dealer must have gone cheap because there were no coffee beans. Even though the dog could not on his or her oath state the fact that the package contained a proscribed drug, I accepted the affidavit of the postal inspector that he believed the dog was reputable and had the necessary expertise as the dog had shown satisfactory performance in a narcotics detection training program and in other detections. (See Florida v. Harris 568 U.S. ___, 2013, for approval of issuance of search warrant based upon such an affidavit). I issued the search warrant and upon delivery of the package to the Angola house by the rural mail carrier about ten staked out Deputy Sheriffs, after knocking on the front door and waiting for about ten seconds for a response, broke through the door. The officers were almost late. Most of the hashish was disappearing down the toilet. The propriety of the convictions and the issuance of the search warrant were later upheld on appeal by the Indiana Appellate Court.

The second drug case involved a state police undercover officer who had infiltrated a weapons and drug selling group in Fort Wayne, Indiana. The officer had arranged to purchase a large quantity of cocaine from the group. The exchange of drugs and money was to take place in the Angola Holiday Inn parking lot which was just three miles south of the Michigan state line. The officer waited in his old car in the parking lot at the appointed time. He was wired. Two state police were in a van nearby with radio receivers. Two Steuben County deputy sheriffs were cruising nearby in an unmarked car. Soon a car approached the lot (a raven black 1970 Boss 302 Mustang), circled slowly by all of the parked vehicles, and departed. The officer recognized the driver as one of the group from Fort Wayne. In the front seat was a large Doberman, a status symbol among drug dealers. Then a second drug dealer drove into the lot and pulled up beside the undercover officer. The drug dealer told the officer to get into the dealer's car and they drove away. This was obviously an unanticipated change of plans which was complicated by the fact that the wire was not working. The police were frantic. They did not know where the dealer was taking the officer and thought that his cover may have been blown.

The drug dealer drove north into Michigan and then turned west and south on a gravel road into Indiana. The car stopped and the drug dealer jumped out and uncovered a large package buried in a snow bank. The package was opened by the officer and the cocaine tested while the dealer drove north just over the state line into Michigan. It tested pure cocaine and the officer paid the dealer. All of the time the officer and the dealer were talking the officer assumed that all of the conversations were being overheard by the other police officers. He thought that they were near and would come to his assistance shortly. The officer pulled his hand gun and ordered the dealer to stop the car and get out.

Just then the backup Mustang being driven north out of Indiana appeared and drove toward the officer. The car contained a snarling Doberman and the other dealer, probably armed. The officer with drawn pistol stood in the middle of the road to block the Mustang. The officer did not know what he should do next. He was expecting his own backup. Luckily, the sheriffs, who had been frantically cruising all of the back gravel roads in the area, came upon the scene and helped subdue both of the dealers. The Doberman was thankfully spared and tied to a tree. A search of both vehicles disclosed more coke and several semi-automatic weapons. Both dealers were charged in Indiana and Michigan with possession of unregistered firearms, possession and sale of cocaine. The defendants claimed the defense of entrapment-that the idea of committing the crimes originated with the police when the defendants had no previous intention or disposition to break the law. The defendants also claimed that the Indiana officers had no right to arrest them in Michigan and that the officers had no probable cause to arrest. The defendant who was in the first car filed a motion, based upon entrapment, to dismiss the case and to exclude all evidence of the drugs and guns as improperly obtained in Michigan. I denied the motion. The backup defendant, who was represented by the same defense attorney, then procured a change of venue to another judge and filed the same motion before the new judge. The new judge, who was the Circuit Court judge of an adjoining county, granted the motion and dismissed the case against the backup defendant. In the trial of the first defendant before me the jury deliberated only one hour. The jury convicted the defendant of all three crimes and I sentenced him to ten years in prison. Prior to the trial, the defendant was offered a plea bargain by the prosecutor which would have called for a total sentence of two years. The defendant refused such offer. His well paid attorney had assured him that he would get him off scot free! The conviction was upheld on appeal to the Indiana Appellate Court.

My only personal brush with the criminal law illustrates the fact that sometimes the complexities of constitutional protections do not filter down to the lower levels of police enforcement. After retiring from the bench I stopped briefly at my old law office one day. I parked right in front of the office. I looked out the front window and observed a lady Angola City Police officer placing a large yellow chalk mark on my right rear tire, writing something on

219

a tablet and walking away. The object of the marking was to keep tabs on parked cars to see if they violated a city ordinance against parking over two hours. I promptly went to my car and started to rub the yellow mark off. The officer came running back to my car and told me that I could not do that. I said that I had just parked my car, was about to leave and as she knew I was not violating any parking ordinance. She said that she would have to give me a parking ticket because I had rubbed some chalk off and I was not supposed to do this. She gave me a parking ticket. After receiving the ticket I went to talk to the Angola Chief of Police. I asked him if there was any ordinance or other law which forbad rubbing off yellow chalk marks on tires. He said that there was no such ordinance or law but they had been having problems with people doing that and he had instructed his officers to ticket any such action. Somewhat dismayed, I asked him if I had heard him correctly. Did he really instruct his officers to issue misdemeanor traffic citations to persons who had not violated any law? He said yes. He did so because something had to be done to stop the illegal excess parking. I asked what would be done if I did not pay the $2.00 fine for violating a law that did not exist. He said with a straight face that if I did not pay the fine within 24 hours he would follow procedure and instruct the City Attorney to file charges against me in Circuit Court for the $2.00 plus $25.00 per day late penalty. I paid the $2.00.

In 1971 I faced a decision which would test my basic beliefs as to the right of privacy and the treatment of persons with mental disabilities.

The Steuben County Welfare Department filed a petition to have an eighteen year old woman under their care and custody involuntarily sterilized. The petition alleged that she was "feebleminded", was about to be married to a man who was also feebleminded whom she had met at a mental institution, and that if not sterilized she would most likely have several children of like mental condition. The petition was pursuant to Indiana law and asked that a hearing date be set for the presentation of evidence and that notice be given to the eighteen year old woman.

This procedure and authority for a judge to order sterilization was set forth in an Indiana 1927 statute. The Indiana statute was based upon a Virginia statute which had been upheld by the United States Supreme Court in *Buck v. Bell* (1927). The statute gave a judge after a proper hearing the right to order sterilization of an institutionalized male or female if the judge determined that the respondent was "feebleminded or morally delinquent."

Buck v. Bell involved Carrie Buck, an eighteen year old girl, who was declared to be "a genetic threat to society" by a Virginia state court judge. According to the judge's decision, Carrie was the daughter of "a socially inadequate mother and the mother herself of a similarly afflicted daughter." Justice Oliver Wendell Holmes, Jr. of the United States Supreme Court wrote the opinion of the court. The opinion stated, "It is better for all of the world, if instead of waiting to execute degenerate offspring for crime, or to let them starve for their imbecility, society can prevent those who are manifestly unfit from continuing their kind. The principle that sustains compulsory vaccination is broad enough to cover cutting Fallopian tubes....Three generations of imbeciles are enough!" The Supreme Court never reversed this decision. Thirty-three states including Indiana passed laws similar to the Virginia law authorizing involuntary sterilization. These state laws were all repealed by the mid 1970s and Indiana repealed its law in 1974. Two thousand three hundred men and women were involuntarily sterilized in Indiana and over sixty-five thousand nationwide.

When the petition was filed with me, I did not set a hearing date. I asked the Welfare Department to withdraw the petition and stated to the director of the Welfare Department that even though the Indiana law authorized such a procedure, I would never issue an involuntary sterilization order. The Welfare Department deferred to my decision.

There is a footnote to this issue. In *Stump v. Sparkman* (1978), the United States Supreme Court upheld a 1971 decision by the judge of the DeKalb Circuit Court (the Circuit Court judge of the county adjoining Steuben County) which authorized the sterilization of a fifteen year old girl. The court held that the judge was immune from any liability for his decision ordering the sterilization since it was a "judicial decision." The facts of the case are startling. The girl's mother petitioned the judge to issue an order to have her daughter sterilized. The petition alleged:

"Ora Spitler McFarlin, being duly sworn upon her oath states that she is the natural mother of and has custody of her daughter, Linda Spitler, age fifteen (15) being born January 24, 1956 and said daughter resides with her at 108 Iwo Street, Auburn, DeKalb County, Indiana.

Affiant states that her daughter's mentality is such that she is considered to be somewhat retarded although she is attending or has attended the public schools in DeKalb Central School System and has been passed along with other children in her age level even though she does not have what is considered normal mental capabilities and intelligence. Further, that said affiant has had problems in the home of said child as a result of said daughter leaving the home on several occasions to associate with older youth or young men and as a matter of fact having stayed overnight with said youth or men and about which incidents said affiant did not become aware of until after such incidents occurred. As a result of this behavior and the mental capabilities of said daughter, affiant believes that it is to the best interest of said child that a Tubal Ligation be performed on said minor daughter to prevent unfortunate circumstances to occur and since it is impossible for the affiant as mother of said minor child to maintain and control a continuous observation of the activities of said daughter each and every day."

The petition and subsequent order were never officially filed with the court. There was no hearing and no evidence was submitted to the judge. The girl was not notified that the petition had been filed and the judge did not appoint any attorney or guardian-ad-litem to represent the girl. The petition was granted the same day that it was submitted to the judge. The girl was told by her mother that she was going to have her appendix removed. Two years later the daughter was married and upon failure to become pregnant she learned for the first time that she had been sterilized. She and her husband sued the judge, the doctors and the hospital for damages. Based upon the Supreme Court decision, recovery was denied.

The implications of this decision are frightening. The immense power given Indiana circuit and superior court judges makes it imperative that only qualified judges, both in legal training and moral character, be elected. Great power should always be exercised with great restraint.

13. The case of *Miranda v. Arizona* (1966) is an example of the practical workings of the due process clause. We all have watched crime dramas where the police are always giving a suspected criminal "his Miranda rights." In the *Miranda* case the police after a vigorous and prolonged interrogation of the accused obtained a confession. Miranda claimed that the police should have told him of his constitutional rights to be silent (Fifth Amendment) and to have an attorney present at the interrogation (Sixth Amendment). The state claimed that even though the Fifth and Sixth Amendments applied to a state criminal charge by virtue of the Fourteenth Amendment due process clause, Arizona law and the Constitution did not require such advice prior to interrogation. Miranda claimed that to be advised of such rights was required to provide a "fundamentally fair procedure" required under procedural due process. Anyone who watches television knows how the Supreme Court ruled. That is why Roberts was read his rights prior to his interrogation. Note: Miranda was subsequently tried again without the confession being admitted and was again found guilty and sentenced to 20-30 years in prison. He was stabbed to death in a bar fight in 1976.

Two other Supreme Court decisions are also good examples of federally protected first eight amendment rights being incorporated in the Fourteenth Amendment due process clause and thereby binding upon the states.

In *Mapp v. Ohio* (1961) Dollree Mapp was convicted of possession of obscene materials seized by the police after breaking down the door of her home. The police were searching for a suspected bombing fugitive. They did not find any fugitive but did find in a drawer in a dresser in her basement some obscene magazines. They did not have a search warrant. A warrant was not required by Ohio law, by federal law or federal court decisions. The Ohio Supreme Court upheld the conviction. The United States Supreme Court decided that this was an unreasonable search and seizure without a warrant, that the seized materials should therefore be excluded from evidence, that the right to not be subjected to such a search was a fundamental right as required by the Fourth Amendment and was incorporated in the Fourteenth Amendment. The charges were therefore dismissed. Dollree was arrested, tried and convicted nine years later after police (with a search warrant) found drugs in her apartment.

In *Gideon v. Wainwright* (1963) Gideon was charged with burglary in a Florida court and he requested the court to appoint an attorney for him as he was indigent. The judge refused. Florida law did not require that an attorney be appointed for an indigent criminal defendant. Federal law and federal court decisions also did not require the appointment of an attorney. He was tried, convicted and sentenced to five years in jail. Gideon sent a hand written letter directly to the United States Supreme Court asking that they intervene. The Supreme Court allowed the letter to be filed as an appeal and appointed Abe Fortas, himself soon to be named a Justice of the Court, to represent Gideon. The Supreme Court decided that Gideon had a right to have an attorney appointed for him, that such a right was a fundamental right, and that this Sixth

Amendment fundamental right was incorporated in the Fourteenth Amendment. The conviction was vacated and the Florida court was ordered to provide Gideon with an attorney upon any retrial. At his subsequent trial, represented by an attorney, Gideon was acquitted.

Before *Mapp* (1961), *Gideon* (1963) and Miranda (1966), in some states, a person charged with a serious felony could have been convicted based upon evidence seized from his home without a search warrant, was not entitled to a court appointed attorney to help defend him if he could not afford an attorney, and any confession obtained after a long and vigorous interrogation could be used against him without being advised of his right to remain silent. Such actions did not violate the Constitution of the United States.

Indiana courts interpreted the Indiana Constitution as early as 1854 as requiring that an indigent criminal defendant be furnished an attorney at public expense for all felonies, and as early as 1923 as requiring that evidence obtained pursuant to an invalid search warrant or no search warrant be excluded.

FURTHER AFFIANT SAYETH NAUGHT

29780630R00125

Made in the USA
Lexington, KY
03 February 2019